THE WATER
GARDEN

LESLIE GEDDES-BROWN

THE WATER
GARDEN

MERRELL
LONDON · NEW YORK

To Hew, as always

First published 2008 by Merrell Publishers Limited

Head office:
81 Southwark Street
London SE1 0HX

New York office:
740 Broadway, Suite 1202
New York, NY 10003

merrellpublishers.com

British Library Cataloguing-in-Publication data:
Geddes-Brown, Leslie
The water garden
1. Water gardens
I. Title
635.9'674

ISBN-13: 978-1-8589-4410-4
ISBN-10: 1-8589-4410-4

Produced by Merrell Publishers Limited
Design concept by Maggi Smith
Layout by Martin Lovelock
Picture-researched by Emily Hedges
Copy-edited by Caroline Ball
Proof-read by Sarah Yates
Indexed by Hilary Bird

Printed and bound in Singapore

Acknowledgements

Creating a book is not always enjoyable. I say
'creating' because a book involves far more than
just writing: a structure must be found, illustrations
chosen and a design worked out, all to the
satisfaction of not only the author but also the
editors, picture researchers, proof-reader, designers,
publisher and, one hopes, the reader. Not always a
happy experience.

But *The Water Garden* has gone swimmingly from
the first. So, a raised glass (not of water) to Julian
Honer, Rosanna Fairhead, Emily Hedges, Caroline
Ball, Paul Arnot, Nick Wheldon, Michelle Draycott
and everyone else involved, not least my agent,
Gillian Vincent, friend and fountain of knowledge.

Front jacket
Ninfa, Latina, Italy (see pages 87–89).

Back jacket
Top row, left to right
Jardin Majorelle, Marrakesh, Morocco (see
pages 42–45); Temple of Music, West Wycombe Park,
Buckinghamshire (see page 69); Stiteler Garden,
Arizona (see pages 182–83); The Smith Residence,
Sydney, Australia (see pages 139–41).
Bottom row, left to right
Fallingwater, Pennsylvania (see pages 154–57); Schloss
Wörlitz, Sachsen-Anhalt, Germany (see pages 71–73);
West Lake, Hangzhou, China (see pages 27–29);
Peterhof, Gulf of Finland, Russia (see pages 54–57).

Frontispiece
Kathryn Gustafson, Jardins de l'Imaginaire, Terrasson,
Dordogne, France.

CONTENTS

INTRODUCTION

So, what is a water garden? There are the obvious gardens, Versailles at their head, that would be nothing at all without water because their fountains and pools and canals are more important than any other feature to their design and enjoyment. Then there are gardens that use natural water features as part of their beauty: lakes and streams, rivers and waterfalls, clifftops overlooking wild seas and islands surrounded by oceans or lakes.

It could be argued that water is a component of every garden: even in dry gravel gardens the plants thrive because they are secretly nurtured by moisture under the stones. Water and nutrients are the two essentials to plants, and hydroponics means that even soil can be done away with. However, this book is all about how water comes to the aid of the gardener, not as an essential to plant life but in garden design, as a visible, participatory element. So, bog gardens are not included here, although I was tempted by Derek Jarman's Prospect Cottage in Kent (even though he included no water feature among the planting at all), because his garden owes its entire character to its position by the sea.

Virtually every style of gardening throughout history has relied on water as an essential decorative element, from the cooling rills of the Persian paradise garden to the naturalistic landscaping of vast, man-made lakes from Hangzhou to Stowe. Styles have ranged from the formal fountain gardens of the Renaissance to wild gardens beside rushing Scottish burns where Victorian gardeners tried to imitate a rhododendron-shrouded Himalayan ravine, to Japanese gardens where dry river beds and cascades are constructed without water. There are gardens with gigantic cascades, whether real or man-made, such as that at Powerscourt in Ireland and the hugely impressive one in the Swedish botanic garden in Gothenburg. Water gardens also created their own architecture: boathouses, pavilions and bridges, as well as such conceits as shell-lined caves and grottoes that were popular from Painshill to Pratolino.

Above Versailles, designed by André Le Nôtre for Louis XIV, the Sun King, was immediately copied by the grandees of Europe.

Opposite The waterfall at Powerscourt is the highest in all Ireland, adding a wild, romantic grandeur. Variations in land levels encourage gravity-fed jets and cascades.

Having visited the Royal Horticultural Society's Chelsea Flower Show over the decades, I have noticed that now, after a period of lack of interest, there is a revival of enthusiasm for water gardens. This may be a result of climate change and ever hotter summers, or the development of the technology that makes waterfalls, modernistic fountains and other watery effects easy to achieve. The best garden in the show of 2000 (a very good year for show gardens), 'Evolution' by Piet Oudolf and Arne Maynard, featured an arching jet of water that leapt from one pool to another (overleaf); anyone wandering in would have been drenched, but clearly this did not deter the judges.

I shall be looking at how famous designers have used water features in the past, from Bernardo Buontalenti, architect and designer to the Medicis, to 'Capability' Brown, a major mover in the landscape gardens of England, along with the more recent contributions of Sir Geoffrey Jellicoe, Frank Lloyd Wright and Ian Hamilton Finlay. I shall be looking, too, at how designers, often confined to small urban spaces, have nonetheless found it possible to include just one small fountain or a single still pool. The influence of the traditional water gardens of the Far East and of Islamic cultures from India to Spain is huge, especially on designers who are working in town gardens or in arid areas, as the heavy reliance on stone, bamboo, infinity pools, silent rills and trickling troughs shows. Included here, too, are those gardens linked to a large expanse of water that cannot be disregarded: gardens beside lakes and rivers, gardens perched on cliffs and by maritime inlets, and island gardens, where water is literally omnipresent.

Of course, water today is a political subject: if global warming continues we are likely to have too little in certain areas and too much in others. Water will probably become a resource that we have to use with care rather than with abandon. But the very fact that it will be important and valuable will increase its worth in our eyes. When I consider the efforts made by past civilizations to get water to where it was needed (see pages 10–13), I foresee that great ingenuity will be used to bring water to future gardens.

Nor need we be cavalier with a precious resource: a little water can go a long way. Cycled and recycled, the same water can gush down cascades, ooze under boggy plants and shoot up in fountains, then lie still in ponds or lakes before setting off again to rejoin nature's streams and rivers. It is all the same water, losing little substance except through evaporation. And, should electricity- or oil-fed pumps fail, the laws of gravity and mechanics can be put to use as they were in the past. History should teach us that there is nothing wrong with enjoying a rare resource for its beauty.

Opposite, top Best in show at Chelsea in 2000, 'Evolution' was designed by Piet Oudolf and Arne Maynard and featured high-tech water jets.

Opposite, bottom Mirror-like stretches of water reflect the monumental architecture of the palace at Fatehpur Sikri, India.

Left Water gardening has created its own architecture, such as this unassuming boathouse on the lake at Rofford Manor, Oxfordshire.

Below, left Ornamental bridges are a charming as well as practical element of a well-planned water garden. This one is at Bodnant in Wales.

Below, right Where would water gardens be without a grotto and attendant water god?

9

From prehistory onwards, humans have always lived near water, and from earliest times water was seen as more than just a basic element that sustained life and allowed crops to grow. Rowland Parker, in his fine book *The Common Stream* (1975), which charts the life of a Cambridgeshire village, put it in a nutshell: 'every spring of water and every stream born of those springs was the object of veneration by groups of primitive men who knew, as surely and instinctively as the birds and beasts still know, though most men have forgotten, that the water of those springs and streams was Life itself … . Every village, not just in East Anglia but all over the world, owed its original location in part at least to the proximity or availability of water.'

Springs and streams, it was believed, were inhabited by nymphs and goddesses – always female because they gave people fertile lands – and it was not a huge leap from worshipping the nymph of the spring to beautifying the spot from which the water sprang. Springs were surrounded with decorations, sculpture or depictions of the nymph or goddess. People gave presents to her. Well-dressing, still carried out in Derbyshire, was originally a rite to please the goddess, and the beautiful carvings on wellheads in Venice or on Anglican fonts are an extension of this.

Of all the natural phenomena, the laws governing water are perhaps the easiest to understand. One does not have to know why something happens, just that it does and it always will. Water's laws are immutable: at rest it will always be level; it will always flow downhill; and it will always seek the easiest way to do so. Anyone who has tried forcibly to break these rules knows this to his or her cost. The predictable behaviour of water, probably understood from prehistory, has made it possible for people to create wide pools within streams for fish, dam areas to create a reservoir (even beavers know this one), drive mill wheels and, in more recent times, derive energy. Water has also proved to be an effective defence and a natural frontier.

It is a short step from creating a millpond to appreciating the dead-flat calm of the still pond mirroring the passing clouds in the sky. Then people would contrast this peaceful surface with the flash and dash of the water as it crashed through the mill race, the energetic thunder of falling water and the way water drops caught the sun as they cascaded off the wheel's blades. Here, in essence, were all the elements of an ideal water garden, with the still pond signifying serenity and the racing, falling water the energy of nature. When it came to laying out gardens, gardeners understood how the natural laws controlling water could be harnessed and how water could be put to use to beautify their work.

In the world of the ancient desert civilizations – the Egyptians, Sumerians and Assyrians – water was highly valued because it was so scarce. In Mesopotamia, the land between the rivers, the Tigris and the Euphrates were life-sustainers in a parched region. A cuneiform tablet from Mesopotamia, dating from 4000 BC, describes how the water god, Enki, told the sun god, Utu, to allow fresh water on to the desert to create a garden of fruit trees and meadows. Unfortunately, when divine intervention did not work, men had to invent their own machines to transport water from wells, rivers and oases to barren areas. Water was essential to life, but people came to love the psychologically cooling sounds of trickling water or splashing fountains. No garden in any parched area was ever created without water features.

In Mesopotamian Assyria in the seventh century BC, water was brought to Sennacherib's garden in Nineveh by an aqueduct that was fed by a swamp, which, coincidentally, was also a source of food such as wildfowl. Water was also brought to Nineveh around this time by diverting mountain streams. 'To dam the flow of water, I made a pond and planted reeds in it,' recorded Sennacherib. In the same region, Nebuchadnezzar II, who lived until about 562 BC, was the probable creator of the Hanging

Gardens of Babylon, one of the seven wonders of the ancient world. A screw system brought water up from the River Euphrates to irrigate the terraces.

Throughout the Persian Empire, extensive networks of underground aqueducts (*qanats*), some of them tiled to stop seepage, were built to store water and prevent it from evaporating in the blazing sun. The *qanats* fed reservoirs and *jubes* (irrigation channels), from which water seeped directly to the roots of favoured plants. Beds were made below the level of the ground so that, when water was released, they would be watered first.

In Egypt, irrigation systems made use of the seasonal flood waters of the Nile. During the floods, water was collected behind dykes for pools, canals and wells to be used in the dry season. Flood plains were also used for agriculture in sub-Saharan Africa. Great herds of ruminants would overgraze the

land in dry areas, but when the floods came the land would suddenly be revived. When the water drained away, grass would reappear as if by magic and the buffalo would be herded back on to the plains.

In all these regions, water gardens were highly valued and small amounts of water made to work hard. Cultivated gardens were mostly small, walled and formal. The typical Persian gardens – the fact that their name in Persian gives us the word 'paradise' is an indication of how much they were treasured – were divided into four beds by straight rills of water. The style spread throughout the Arabic world, including Moorish Spain, and travelled east to India with the Mughals. The gardens of the Roman Empire also came to be inspired by this architectural formality. Typically, they would consist of formal beds bounded by canals and rills, and fountains in courtyards surrounded by shady pillared walks. The Romans, of course, were masters in the use of water. The ambitious and impressive aqueducts and watercourses they built all over the empire, many of which survive, brought water incredible distances from mountain springs and lakes to towns

Using calm water as a mirror is an effect that has been deployed by gardeners and designers for centuries. This stretch of water reflects a pavilion of the Banque Générale de Luxembourg; its garden was designed by Jacques Wirtz.

and villas that had inadequate supplies of their own. They also constructed early spas, such as Bath (which they knew as Aquae Sulis, 'the waters of Sulis'). Whereas the early Britons knew about and had worshipped at this source of natural hot water with curative powers, the Romans used it as the basis for building a sophisticated town, channelling the spring into the large baths that still attract people today.

The monasteries that sprang up after the Dark Ages took their lead from the Roman concept of a garden. Cloisters, shaded by roofs held by ornate columns, surrounded a courtyard open to the sky, where plants would grow around a central wellhead. These were not pleasure gardens as we understand them, but were intended to help meditation and induce serenity among the orders of monks and nuns.

It is not fanciful to see the same stylistic lineage travelling from ancient Mesopotamia via Rome, Moorish Spain and medieval monasteries to the Renaissance gardens of Europe in the sixteenth and seventeenth centuries. Water was invariably controlled in canals, rectangular pools and ornate fountains. None of these styles of water garden allowed the least inkling of natural asymmetry or wildness: that would not make an appearance in Western gardens until the eighteenth century.

By contrast, the ancient civilizations of China and Japan liked their water gardens to have at least a semblance of nature. Here, water in the garden had a quite different tradition. Although vast areas of China are desert or near-desert, its population is concentrated in areas where water is plentiful; for many Chinese, flood was (and still is) a greater concern than drought. Rain and the waters of huge rivers created a softer, greener environment. Water was channelled into irrigation systems for growing rice in paddy fields and, later, to provide the water for great landscaping projects involving huge lakes and intricate water gardens.

Japanese gardens were highly influenced by Chinese naturalism, but on a smaller scale. Lakes and pools were beautified by carefully naturalistic planting, and the creation of picturesque islets and tiny cascades was raised to the level of an art form. As in China, water was spiritually significant, so its presence, whether literal or metaphorical, was a key element in every garden.

In China, the original impetus for creating large-scale naturalistic landscape parks was to attract mythical beings, the Immortals, who were believed to hold the secret of eternal life. The Immortals liked beautiful lakes, mountainous backdrops, cascades and wooded islands, and Chinese gardeners tried to simulate these, even in towns.

The first emperor of China, Qin Shi Huang Di, set out around 210 BC on a tour of his vast empire to find an Immortal or two, but, ironically, died en route. Before he died, however, Qin Shi

Above Persian gardens followed a traditional layout, being walled and split by four rills meeting at a central pond.

Opposite, top The Assyrian king Sennacherib was heavily involved in his garden's design. This carving of his garden at Nineveh dates from around 645 BC.

Opposite, bottom Chinese scholars and poets, such as Wang Yuyang, the poet pictured in this seventeenth-century scroll, needed and appreciated the serenity and seclusion of their gardens.

Huang Di had already made his own garden, park and hunting reserve, planting it with rare specimens brought back from different regions of his varied domain. The ambitious scale of these early imperial water features was possible because, as early as the fifth century BC, Chinese scholars had worked out water tables and how to use gravity to move the water.

As a result of these discoveries, the lands of both Islam and Europe were able to use gravity to astonishing effect, most notably in the sixteenth-century garden of the Villa d'Este in Italy (see pages 59–61). From Italy, the Classical Renaissance style, with its perfect proportion and symmetry and exuberant use of water, spread in the following century across Europe, particularly to France, where André Le Nôtre (1613–1700) orchestrated the astonishing gardens at Versailles and Saint-Cloud for the Sun King, Louis XIV, and his family. The monumental 90-metre (295-foot) cascade designed by Antoine Le Pautre at Saint-Cloud still survives, as does the twenty-four-step cascade at Chatsworth in Derbyshire, designed by M. Grillet, a pupil of Le Nôtre, for the Duke of Devonshire at the very end of the seventeenth century.

The last truly magnificent water gardens made in Western Europe were those of the landscape and Romantic movements. If the formal water gardens of the Mediterranean and the Near East were the inspiration for the formal gardens of sixteenth- and seventeenth-century Europe, then it is likely that the naturalistic

gardens of China were one of the inspirations for the landscaped gardens of eighteenth-century England.

Constructing an ideal landscape meant a lot of heavy labour by peasants, and a long timescale for excavating great lakes, reshaping the contours of the land and diverting rivers. Then came the embellishments, inspired by the Classical landscape paintings of Claude Lorrain (1600–1682) and Gaspard Poussin (1615–1675). Garden buildings included boathouses, belvederes and fishing pavilions, either set on the water for the enjoyment of those using them, or carefully placed as eye-catchers to be viewed from afar. The Classical proportions of the sixteenth-century architect Andrea Palladio were a favourite style, but a taste for the oriental in the eighteenth century led to wooden chinoiserie bridges, small Japanese-style tea-houses and approximations of pagodas. Parties would saunter around these artfully contrived landscapes, enjoying the 'natural' scenery, and encountering a carefully ruined folly or a grotto (sometimes complete with hermit).

As the eighteenth century moved into the nineteenth, tastes turned towards a greater appreciation of nature for itself. Such rugged, untamed areas as the Scottish Highlands and the Swiss Alps lost their threatening image and became instead grand examples of Romantic Nature. The previously forbidding Lake District, in the north of England, was transformed in people's minds into a natural idyll once it could be seen through the eyes and verse of the Lakeland poets, prime movers in the Romantic movement, who would fell-walk with the best of them. Of course, nature was not really left completely untamed, and Romantic gardens were an idealized, controlled version of 'the wild'. When the artist and writer John Ruskin (see page 116) lived at Brantwood on the shores of Lake Coniston, he had made for him a 'gondola', which, with the aid of a motor, would travel around the lake. (The National Trust has now re-created this, and his enjoyment of the lakeside from the centre of the water can be appreciated by anyone who pays for a ticket [opposite].)

Left, top Cascades do not need chasms. Chatsworth's dignified version is on near-level land.

Left, middle and bottom Diplomatic and trade missions to China fired a taste for chinoiserie in the eighteenth and early nineteenth centuries, although, as this eighteenth-century drawing (middle) by Thomas Robins demonstrates, the Western version lost something in translation. This bridge (below) is at Heale House, Wiltshire.

Opposite, top Water was a vital ingredient for designers of landscape gardens, and William Kent was lucky to have the River Cherwell on hand at Rousham, Oxfordshire.

Opposite, bottom Writer and artist John Ruskin had a motorized 'gondola' in which to ply Lake Coniston beside his lakeside home, Brantwood.

The arrival of the Industrial Revolution brought another change in humans' relationship with nature, and the enjoyment of water in the garden seems to have declined. My theory is that once what had been a sign of luxury and conspicuous consumption became available to the masses through the advent of steam – and later electric – power, it lost its appeal. It was just no longer impressive to create a 150-metre (500-foot) fountain when it could all be done with the flick of a switch. The Victorians came to look for other ways of creating spectacle, such as enormously intricate, labour-intensive flower beds of annuals grown in huge greenhouses by regiments of gardeners. While water still featured, in ponds and fountains, it was not the main event.

It is difficult to think of any major twentieth-century gardens where water was the prime element in the design. As the landscape garden might claim to be Britain's main contribution to global garden design, and 'English-style' gardens in other countries would be unthinkable without their rivers, canals or lakes, it is curious that the great English gardens of the late nineteenth and twentieth centuries are not known for their water features. Such gardens as Sissinghurst in Kent, Nymans in Sussex, and Hidcote in Gloucestershire, and the work of Gertrude Jekyll and Sir Edwin Lutyens, Rosemary Verey and

15

Christopher Lloyd, all lack imposing watery elements. Cottage gardens, rock gardens, Himalayan gardens, and gardens with 'rooms' and herbaceous borders were all praised and popular instead, and, while visitors to the Chelsea Flower Show were regularly regaled until the 1980s with splashing falls of water apparently spouting from Welsh slate, these did not catch the imagination of either gardeners or the public.

It is only lately that water features have become popular again, perhaps because of concerns about climate change allied to the fact that new technology makes all sorts of fancies available. Formal cascades, which virtually vanished from England with the advent of the landscape movement, have returned at select locations (see page 53), and in the United States Lawrence Halprin is among those who have created notable modern examples. The show gardens created for the millennium at the Chelsea Flower Show were all about water, and since then there has not been a show where it was not featured. Perhaps we have come to realize that we do not, after all, need a landscaped park to enjoy water in all its varied forms.

When lakes and rivers were essential to the fashionable garden, the formal set piece of rills and fountains became old hat.

Today that style has been revived, with many a Campagna urn overflowing into a formal pond, even in town gardens. Rills, canals and black-lined rectangular pools are being constructed once again, and the stone troughs and bamboo spouts of the Far East are proving perennially popular. It would seem that even the Romantic idyll of spumes of wild water crashing over Welsh slate is ready for a revival.

Opposite, top left Water often features in show gardens at the Chelsea Flower Show. This neat waterfall in 1999 demonstrated a modern style of small-scale, controlled cascade.

Opposite, top right This sinuous rill is one of the most memorable of William Kent's water features in the gardens at Rousham, Oxfordshire.

Opposite, bottom, and above Contemporary water gardens rely on modern materials and simple foliage, such as bamboo.

Right This homage to Carolus Linnaeus by Ulf Nordfjell won a gold medal at Chelsea in 2007.

THE ORIENTAL WATER GARDEN

The Chinese have a saying: if you want to be happy for a week, take a wife; if you want to be happy for a month, kill a pig; but if you want to be happy for ever, create a garden. This is a proverb that they have always taken seriously, from the emperor down. The as yet unbreached tomb of the first emperor (see pages 12–13) is reputed to contain a representation of the Earth, complete with trees and meadows in precious metals and jewels and the empire's great rivers re-created in flowing mercury. By the time of the great Han emperor Wudi (140–87 BC) the character of the Chinese garden, as nature in microcosm, was set.

Wudi became obsessed with the Immortals, who were thought to live in a mountain fastness and possess a potion that endowed the drinker with eternal youth. When he failed to track them down, he set out instead to create a great park filled with man-made hills, lakes and islands that would entice the Immortals to him. Although the Immortals were not seduced by this vision, the Chinese people were, and Chinese gardens are still made in this pattern.

For some, this re-creation of the natural landscape became an extremely expensive passion, and families, officials and even emperors were brought to bankruptcy, exile and death. The merchant Yuan Guanhau made himself just such an ambitious garden, following the emperor's style, excavating lakes, diverting streams and capturing wild beasts. This was too much for the emperor, who executed the presumptuous merchant for his extravagance. The Han dynasty (206 BC–AD 220) presided over a great expansion of the empire, which brought new plants into Chinese gardens: the traveller Zhang Qian is credited with introducing vines and probably tea to China, and because paper was also invented during this period, records survive of Han gardens.

The exquisite beauty of West Lake in China lies in the serenity of its composition. It is the ideal Chinese water garden.

19

The second Sui emperor, the tyrannical Yangdi (AD 569–618), is famous for his Grand Canal project, which made travel by canal possible from Hangzhou 1800 kilometres (1100 miles) north to Beijing, but he also commanded less practical, but no less grandiose, watery projects, including sixteen 'water palaces' on a 10-kilometre (6-mile) lake dug by a million labourers. Even barbarians were inspired by Chinese gardens. Beijing's extensive Beihai ('Northern Sea') Park is almost half water: a great lake with a man-made island at its centre on which Kublai Khan, grandson of Genghis, built a series of pavilions and palaces. Marco Polo, who visited in the latter part of the thirteenth century, was suitably impressed.

Confucius (551–479 BC) said that wise men found pleasure in water and that water was like a wise man in that it follows its own path, finds its own level and is natural. The Chinese garden, with its mountains, streams and lakes, is Confucian in concept, with water an integral part. Chinese gardens are traditionally composed of four elements: rock, water, buildings and plants. Together these create balance and harmony, with rocks – yang and male – forming the bones of the garden, and water – yin and female – providing the veins. Wang Shizhen, a scholar writing in the sixteenth century about his own garden, described a mountain range, three peaks,

two stone bridges and six wooden ones, four sets of pools and rapids and 'two watercourses for floating wine cups. The various rocky cliffs and rushing streams cannot be counted on one's fingers.'

Even the very poor and those in crowded cities far from lakes or rushing mountain streams sought to have their own water gardens. They created *pen jing*, small bowls in which miniature landscapes of mountains and lakes and small plants provided, on the smallest scale, the same encapsulation of nature as the extensive domains of mandarins and emperors.

Gardens were seen as places of peace and tranquility, somewhere to contemplate nature, providing stillness in an overburdened life – whether that entailed keeping one step ahead in potentially lethal political machinations or the backbreaking toil of a peasant. In a book on garden-making written between 1631 and 1634, Ji Cheng, an artist and landscape designer, counselled against travelling: 'If one can find stillness in the midst of city turmoil, why should one then forego such an easily accessible spot and seek a more distant one?' (*Yuan Ye*, 1634). This could have been written for Yuyuan, a garden of tiny lakes and ponds, bridges and belvederes, a pocket of tranquility in the centre of Shanghai's 'city turmoil'. It is almost enough to tempt the Immortals from their mountains.

When the Japanese Ono no Imoko was sent as a diplomatic envoy to Emperor Yangdi in the early seventh century, he returned inspired by the Chinese landscape gardens he had seen (he later became a priest and founded the first school of *ikebana* flower-arranging in Japan). The idea of a garden as idealized landscape developed in Japan and has flourished there ever since.

Like the Chinese, the Japanese see nature as part of the spirit and the divine. The national religions, Shinto and Buddhism, both emphasize the inner meanings of rocks and stones, plants and water. Water is a constant feature in Japanese gardens, whether in lakes and falls or tiny, still troughs. If the Chinese could create a landscaped water garden for the Immortals in a small bowl, the Japanese have gone one further: they have created dry water gardens. Waterfalls and streams exist as though there were water, but these conduits are dry, the water illusory, with instead 'streams' of raked gravel. The symbolism, the imagery, is all. Penelope Hobhouse, in *The Story of Gardening* (2002), says that the large, antique stones so venerated by Japanese gardeners should be seen on a par with the venerable oaks and other champion trees of parks and gardens in the West.

Both Chinese and Japanese styles of gardening have had a huge influence on the West at different times. When the much-travelled diplomat and garden enthusiast Sir William Temple (1628–1699) returned from China, his tales of pagodas and artificial landscapes led to an outbreak of chinoiserie throughout Europe. A century later Londoners flocked to see Sir William Chambers's ten-storey pagoda in Kew Gardens, and oriental wooden bridges and pavilions reflected in carefully naturalistic pools became a fashionable eighteenth-century garden feature. The series of fanciful gardens at Biddulph Grange in Staffordshire, created when Victorian plant-hunting was at its height, included settings appropriate for the new exotics. In 'China', a gaudy Chinese temple stands guard over a water-lily pool.

The Japanese style has had a particularly strong influence on smaller city gardens in the West, where Japanese 'world in miniature' simplicity is admirably suited to providing a sense of space where space is at a premium. Londoners and San Franciscans, Berliners and Parisians have adapted the still water trough, the bamboo pipe feeding a rill, the raked gravel and the rustling bamboo to suit their own small plots, and have learnt, as the Japanese did centuries ago, the serenity and special quality that water – or the illusion of water – brings to a garden.

THE ORIENTAL WATER GARDEN

Tenryu-ji
Kyoto, Japan

The water garden at Tenryu-ji is an extraordinary survival. Built and planted in the mid-fourteenth century, it is the living bridge between the Chinese gardens that so inspired the Japanese of the period and the Japanese style itself. It is even thought that the designer might have been Chinese.

Tenryu-ji ('Heavenly Dragon Temple') was founded in 1339 on the site of an imperial villa, and, although a succession of fires means that the present temple buildings are only about a hundred years old, the garden survived the conflagrations and is believed to look much as it did when fashioned by the founding abbot, Muso Soseki. The garden was commissioned by the first Ashikaga shogun, a warlord who had exiled Emperor Godaigo but then created this garden as an apology after the emperor's death, a gesture reminiscent of the penance of Henry II of England after the murder of Thomas à Becket.

The pool in the water garden is about 60 metres (200 feet) long and designed to be viewed from the temple buildings, its stylized rock landscaping echoed by the real hillsides beyond. The rocks are particularly interesting because they are some of the earliest examples of the influences on gardens of Zen Buddhism and the Chinese

Many oriental gardens were designed to be seen from indoors, and Tenryu-ji is no exception.

Song dynasty. On the far, northern side of the lake, there is a waterfall called the Dragon's Gate. This refers to a Chinese legend that tells of a carp swimming up a great waterfall with massive leaps and, when it finally arrived at the top, being turned into a dragon. Like many garden features, the Dragon's Gate waterfall has a (still relevant) political meaning, pointing out the hoops through which bureaucrats had to jump to reach prominence (mandarins in China had to be notable scholars). Water no longer cascades here, but the three tiers of the rocks still clearly suggest a waterfall, complete with the Carp Stone seeming to jump up through the stream.

After his visit to Kyoto in the 1950s, the writer Sacheverell Sitwell (brother to Osbert and Edith) noted in *Bridge of the Brocade Sash* (1959) that the garden had been rebuilt after several fires:

But it does not seem to have been spoilt by that … let us be content with thinking that the lake, whether or not in its present shape, may be due to the hand of that fourteenth century priest [Muso Soseki], who was the first abbot of the temple. It is among the largest lakes in any of the Kyoto gardens. I shall always remember the beautiful heat of the day we saw Tenryuji and the twang and whirring of the grasshoppers like wound up springs of metal, wound up and let go. On the distant waters towards the far bank were masses of water-lily leaves, but the beauty of the Tenryuji is not so much any particular feature of the garden as the wooded hill rising behind it, a hanging wood from which it was impossible to take one's eyes away. … How beautiful it must look in the moonlight.

Opposite The precision of the raked gravel and the stillness of the water are aids to serenity. In autumn the vibrant reds and oranges of the maples are reflected in the lake.

Above, left The apparently natural planting on the lake's borders uses plenty of artifice, not least in hiding it.

Above, right Every aspect of any Japanese garden is carefully considered. This tiny waterfall is beautifully crafted.

Left Water lilies are almost de rigueur in oriental water gardens.

West Lake
Hangzhou, China

For centuries West Lake has been held up as the ideal Chinese landscape. In the thirteenth century, Marco Polo was moved to describe Hangzhou as the 'most enchanting city in the world'; in later centuries emperors, notably the Kangxi Emperor (reigned 1661–1722), made frequent extended visits, and it is still a favourite excursion destination for romantically inclined Chinese. It is a bustling, modern city on the lakeshore, but the peaceful beauty of the expanse of water surrounded by gentle hills remains timeless, evocative of the classical landscapes painted when Hangzhou was the capital of the Southern Song dynasty (1127–1279).

There was once a sea lagoon where West Lake now lies, but the lake itself is probably man-made, floods from the nearby Qiantang River having been harnessed to create a landscaped lake of great beauty. The lake, which extends over 500 hectares (1235 acres), is crossed by two long causeways, one running from the south to the north shore virtually in a straight line, and the other looping along the north-west shore, taking in Solitary Hill island with its Crane Pavilion. The second causeway is the older, built more than a thousand years

West Lake's causeways, bridges and classical style of planting have for centuries provided an idealized Chinese pastoral scene beloved by poets and emperors alike.

27

ago, but later named after the poet Bai Juyi, who was a local governor in Hangzhou. The straight causeway is called the Su Causeway, built by Su Dongpo, governor in Hangzhou in the eleventh century and also famed as a poet. A third causeway, the Yong Gong, is a modern addition, as is the extension of the lake on the west side.

West Lake combines practicality with the traditional Chinese love of beauty and poetry. The Su Causeway is planted with double lines of weeping willows that emerge, gently swaying, from the frequent mists but also help knit together the earth of the causeway, which doubles as a dyke. On the Bai Causeway, willows are joined by flowering peaches, to be enjoyed by the numerous pedestrians who throng the lake. Sir John Barrow, who was with Lord Macartney on his official visit to the Qianlong Emperor in 1793, wrote in his *Travels in China* (1804) that *Hibiscus mutabilis* was conspicuously planted along the shores of West Lake. The Qianlong emperor, who was a frequent visitor to the area, was also responsible for the planting of tea bushes around the Dragon's Well, a short trip into the mountains, and Dragon's Well tea is still acclaimed.

West Lake is dotted with islands, such as Three Pools Mirror the Moon and Serene Island. All along the shores are viewing points long famed for their magical vistas: Sunset Glow of Lei Hill, View Mountain Bridge and Listening to Orioles Singing in Willows, among others. Today, there are jogging routes over the causeways and hotels around the shore, for this is still a much-loved beauty spot. Locals come to practise their t'ai chi, wedding parties pose against romantic backdrops, couples picnic on the banks and others fish in elegant boats.

Right An area of 500 hectares (1235 acres) of water, islands and lakeside planting is given over to visual pleasure, appreciated as much today as it was a thousand years ago.

Below, left Viewing points around the shore and on the islands are favourite places for watching the sun set over the lake.

Below, right Vibrant water lilies add brilliant pools of colour to the misty green of the lake.

Opposite Traditional Chinese upturned roofs (believed to deflect devils) were much copied in the West.

Zhuozheng Yuan
Suzhou, China

Zhuozheng has been variously translated, but this garden is most usually called the Humble Administrator's Garden, after its creator, a retired court examiner called Wang Xianchen. Wang lived and worked at court during the Ming dynasty before retreating to plant this haven between 1506 and 1521. Perhaps the name was sensible at the period, to avoid any suggestion of wealth or arrogance, but this garden is anything but humble. Not only did Wang spend his time and money evolving a garden of great serenity, but also he encouraged artists to come and stay and record its beauties. Among them was Wen Chengming, one of the official Four Great Painters of the Ming dynasty, who left an album of poetry and paintings made during and after his visit.

Suzhou, capital of Jiangsu province, is sometimes called the 'Venice of China', and is famous for its canals and many gardens with pools and lakes. Zhuozheng Yuan is the largest such garden, and half its surface area is water, a series of irregular pools cunningly leading from one to the next in a watery labyrinth. There are small islands, secret pools and streams, bridges forming perfect vistas,

The administrator of Zhuozheng Yuan might have been 'humble', but Wang Xianchen's garden is anything but: it is complex and serene.

and flat, calm areas of water to mirror the sky and, at night, the moon.

Throughout the garden, buildings and paths are arranged according to the Chinese landscape principles of 'facing views' and 'borrowing views', a concept with which landscape gardeners in the West later became familiar. In the major central portion of the garden (called, variously, Humble, Foolish or Unsuccessful Politician's Garden in another effort at conscious modesty), the principal building, the Hall of Distant Fragrance, looks out over the main lake towards two gentle, green islands. These, too, have their own eye-catching buildings: the Pavilion of Fragrant Snow and Glorious Clouds and,

less grandiose, a small gazebo called Waiting for the Frost. Elsewhere, roofed paths meander along the water's edge to other pavilions or picturesque corners with equally evocative names: Blue Waves Water Courtyard, Eighteen Camellias Hall, Celestial Spring Pavilion.

The air is scented with lotuses, and there is a white wisteria: not *Wisteria sinensis* 'Alba', which the plant-hunter Robert Fortune discovered and brought to the West, but one with an equally fine fragrance. Walls provide support for displays of China roses, which grow luxuriantly in the warm climate; some of these are still being classified and introduced into the West. Plants are

established not only in the soil and water but also in decorative pots, such as the azaleas, which are brought out when in flower. In his *Garden Plants of China* (1999), Chinese plant expert Peter Valder commented that the area known as the Spring Home of Begonia was completely begonia-free when he visited it. Perhaps, he speculated, the plants were only brought out when they flowered, or 'maybe the name is a reference to some beautiful but rejected woman whose residence this was'.

The fate of the garden almost ended with Wang: when he died, his son gambled the whole property away in a single night. Since then it has been divided, changed and almost lost, but it has now been carefully restored. The Chinese say that even though this is a grand garden made up of elegant and imposing buildings, the whole area evokes the atmosphere of a local water village. Zhuozheng is seen in China as the quintessence of a water garden.

Opposite Chinese gardens are always complicated. The owners lived from room to room and from house to house.

Above, left Everything in a traditional Chinese garden had significance. Each tree and plant was manicured to suit the overall design.

Left Water takes up as much space as land at Zhuozheng Yuan, with most buildings poised over ponds and streams.

THE ISLAMIC WATER GARDEN

The style of garden that spread with Islam from Mughal India to Moorish Spain evolved long before the Prophet Mohammed was born. It had its genesis in the gardens of ancient Persia, and was in many ways as far removed from the Chinese and Japanese water gardens as it is possible to be. Where the oriental model was all curves in imitation of nature, the Persian garden was disciplined straight lines, and where the oriental emphasis was on foliage, the Persians delighted in brilliant flowers.

Yet although these two ancient garden styles were very different in form, they had much in common in concept. Both the early Chinese and the Persian rulers created walled hunting parks that they stocked, using their vast power and wealth, with exotic species of flora and fauna. Water was an important element in both, providing, in the case of the arid Persian landscape, another statement of wealth and provision of luxury. The palace of Cyrus the Great, the founder of the Persian Empire in the sixth century BC, had gardens fed by a series of aqueducts that brought water from the mountains. When twentieth-century archaeologists excavated the site, Pasargadae, in the south-west of modern Iran, they found intact white limestone-lined rills forming the classic four-square pattern so characteristic of Persian gardens.

This invariable pattern is known as the *chahar bagh* ('four gardens'), and where the rills intersected there might be a platform where the owner and guests could sit, cooled by the moist air and sound of the running water; or there might be a splashing fountain to create the same pleasing ambience. This design can be seen in traditional 'garden carpets', in which depictions of trees, flowers and wildlife are all incorporated within the *chahar bagh* scheme. The fabulous carpet known as the Spring of Khosrow, made for

The Persian-style Bagh-e Shahzadeh in Kerman, Iran, was designed in the 1880s by the governor of Kerman. A cistern stores water from the mountains to the south to feed the pools.

the palace of Ctesiphon in the sixth century AD, reputedly (it was destroyed in about AD 637) showed rills and flower beds, the areas of earth woven of gold thread and water embroidered with crystals.

With the Muslim conquests through the former Persian Empire in the seventh century, the *chahar bagh* became a model for Islamic gardens. The Prophet Mohammed described paradise as a wonderful garden, and the Koran suggests that it is every man's duty to protect nature, for it is divine. The classic layout became infused with symbolism, and the four streams or rills were said to represent the four rivers that flow through Paradise: of water, milk, honey and wine. Byzantine ambassadors to Baghdad in AD 917 wrote of a palace on the banks of the Tigris: 'The new kiosk is a palace in the midst of two gardens. In the centre was an artificial pond, round which flows a stream in a conduit.' It was, said one, better than polished silver.

The style spread with Islam east to India with the Mughals and west through North Africa to Moorish Spain. Today one can still see the ancient pattern echoed in gardens from the Taj Mahal to the Alhambra, and even (via Spanish colonialism) in the mission gardens of the south-west American states.

Islamic gardens are, typically, comparatively small (although a palace complex would have had several), walled and have water as an important feature. As they were generally in deserts or areas where water was highly valuable, they often entailed wonders of hydraulic engineering. Aqueducts, underground conduits and numerous reservoirs brought water from distant rivers or snowy mountain tops to the parched plains. A 14-kilometre (9-mile)

aqueduct channelled water to the many-splendoured but short-lived Andalucían city of Medina Azahara, built near Córdoba. In the tenth century the caliph could enjoy the refreshing delights of pools and fountains throughout the 120-hectare (297-acre) garden of his palace. There were even reputed to be waterworks here powered by ostriches on treadmills.

Fountains and flowing water are a particular joy of these gardens. Water tanks in the hills allowed series of fountains to spout by the force of gravity. A central canal in the garden of Bagh-e Fin, in present-day Iran, was lined with turquoise tiles, looking not unlike a modern swimming pool, and small fountains bubbled along its length. These were fed by a *qanat* (underground conduit) and operated by gravity. At Toledo, in Spain, a garden included a lake with, at its centre, a crystal pavilion on an island. The pavilion's roof held a water tank that allowed water to run down the clear sides of the walls into the lake. The sensation must have been like being inside a waterfall or an ice cube: imagine the wonder of it on a hot summer's day. The *chadar* was another popular feature of Islamic gardens: a sloping waterfall that encouraged peace and serenity (and coolness) and kept the flies away.

These stylized gardens also influenced the form of medieval monastic cloisters and, later, the formal, symmetrical gardens of the seventeenth century. Look at engravings of European 'Islamic' gardens and the difference seems minimal, although European prints were all perspective and detail and rarely included depictions of the ornately dressed, fat princes and their concubines that make Persian and Mughal miniatures so engaging.

Enough of these gardens still exist, especially in Spain, to be appreciated as they would have been at the height of their popularity. In the Persian heartland where it all began, however, some gardens have fared better than others. In *The Road to Oxiana* (1937), Robert Byron wrote of the garden by the Shrine of Niamatullah: 'The purple cushions on the judas trees and a confetti of early fruit-blossom are reflected in a long pool. In the next court is another pool, shaped like a cross and surrounded by formal beds newly planted with irises. It is cooler here. Straight black cypresses, overtopped by the waving umbrellas of quicker-growing pines, throw a deep woody shade.' But then, in a diary entry, he describes more depressingly a garden gone to seed: 'the courtyard: one pollarded tree stump, an empty pond, and a line of washing all dripping with rain, give a new idea of a Persian garden. At the end stood a vaulted summer-house, but just as I put pencil to it, the whole thing collapsed in a heap ... as a building material, the mud of Delijan is unsuited to bad weather.'

Opposite, left Many oriental carpet designs are based on the *chahar bagh*, the classical Persian garden that combines water and flowers in a formal pattern.

Opposite, middle and right The idea of the *chahar bagh* spread to India with the Mughal emperors, and Mughal miniatures of the privileged at leisure frequently include details of garden rills, pools and fountains in the same formal style.

Above and right Water, especially splashing water, is psychologically cooling. At Bagh-e Fin, south of Qom, an ancient Persian garden that was largely restored in the nineteenth century, water spouts and turquoise tiles lining the channels emphasize the water's coolness and provide a visual contrast with the dry, dusty environment.

Nishat Bagh
Kashmir, India

The water garden at Nishat Bagh is unique:
it is unlike any other Mughal garden,
despite being the work of Asaf Khan IV,
who was the grand vizier (and brother-in-
law) of the Mughal Emperor Jehangir
(1605–1627), and despite the fact that it
was close – in distance and in inspiration –
to Jehangir's own garden at Shalimar.

Like Shalimar, Nishat Bagh ('Garden
of Gladness') slopes down towards the
waters of Lake Dal, a site that, with its
distant backdrop of blue mountains
shimmering in the heat of summer or
snow-covered in winter, is one of the most
beautiful spots on earth. While Nishat Bagh
may be livelier and less subtle than Shalimar,
this is what gives it its sublime beauty.

The garden consists of twelve
terraces, one for each sign of the zodiac,
and a large central canal. The canalized
water descends through a series of
cascades and waterfalls into large pools
and flat areas of canal, all of which
contain fountains. At the end of the final
terrace the expanse of the lake takes over,
for this garden, unlike most Eastern
designs, is not enclosed.

The central canal is flanked by lawns
and flower beds, and the whole garden

The garden of Nishat Bagh, dating from the
seventeenth century, is in one of the most beautiful
spots on earth, between Lake Dal and the Himalayas.

Opposite Although this is clearly a Mughal garden, it is far more playful than most, and, rather than being enclosed, the views down the main cascade open up on to the lake itself.

Top left The magnificent mountains provide a breathtaking backdrop.

Above and top right Nishat Bagh is hugely admired – the jewel in Kashmir's crown – and is enjoyed for its frivolity and liveliness, which are more apparent than in most Mughal gardens.

is shaded by a double row of *chinar* trees (*Platanus orientalis*). At the top of the garden is a pleasure pavilion. A delightful Mughal painting in a book of poems of 1663 by Zafar Khan, a governor of Kashmir, depicts a very grand personage (perhaps Asaf Khan himself?) sitting on a golden oriental carpet with his courtiers around him and Nishat Bagh behind. A steep cascade is shown with a pavilion at the top, and on either side of the rushing water are beds of poppies and irises. In

the background is a range of fierce mountains. Another part of the painting shows a series of arched niches built behind the cascade, probably intended for lights. The Mughals apparently made their waterfalls and fountains even more dramatic by putting lamps behind the water to increase the sparkle. These can still be seen at the seventeenth-century garden of Rambagh at Agra.

The garden also has a *zenana*, a special area for women, where two octagonal, three-storey gazebos were built so that ladies could view the lake, the rice paddies and the mountains beyond. There are also special viewing platforms alongside the rushing water.

The Garden Book (2000) is full of praise for this gem of a water garden: 'As the garden has a far steeper ascent than any other Mughal garden, the features have a more dramatic and lively effect: the water cascades faster, the sizes of the chutes are greater. This garden is much louder and visually ostentatious – a radical move away from the subtle and sublime tranquility of most other Mughal garden settings. The site is superb – and a crowning jewel of the Kashmir.'

THE ISLAMIC WATER GARDEN

Jardin Majorelle
Marrakesh, Morocco

Although the Islamic garden appears, at first sight, to be highly formulaic – high-walled and private, bisected by two canals or rills and with four rectangular beds – the work of the French painter Jacques Majorelle (1886–1962) in Marrakesh proves how adaptable even this format can be.

Majorelle was a great traveller in Africa before he arrived in Morocco, where he decided to stay because of his health. He chose to make his home in the beautiful town of Marrakesh, with its clear light and colour and backdrop of the snow-tipped Atlas Mountains, and he settled at the edge of the town in 1919. Morocco was then still a French colony, and much of the architecture outside the souk and dramatic main square is recognizably French.

The artist, having moved into his pavilion villa with adjoining studio, started to experiment with his walled garden. The garden was already constructed along classic Islamic lines, with its crossing rills, fountains and a large fish tank, and as the garden was built on a sloping site, there were constant changes in level as the main path wound its way through the flower beds. However, it was only in the 1930s that the garden began to take on its distinctive character.

Majorelle was created by, and named after, the French painter Jacques Majorelle, who settled in Marrakesh.

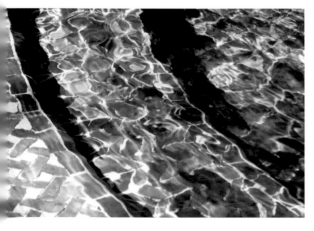

Opposite Majorelle blue, the deep cobalt blue used throughout the garden, features here in an intricately tiled design for a pool.

Top left The garden combines strict 'bones' in its structure with wonderfully wild and exotic planting.

Top right A magical double contrast: stark dry spikes seen through a fountain's spray and Majorelle blue glowing out of the surrounding greenery.

Above The Moors knew all about the tricks of light and shade and watery reflections long before David Hockney captured them in his paintings.

The Mexican artist Luis Barragán (1902–1988) is often cited as the prime mover in exotically painted exteriors, but Majorelle was well in advance of him. In 1933 he started to paint the hardware of the garden in the strongest possible colours, their hues sharpened under the glaring Moroccan sun and brilliant blue sky. The ironwork, windows and plant pots were painted chrome-yellow, the doors apple-green and the paths shades of red, pink and blue, echoing the exterior adobe walls, which were in the traditional Marrakesh pink. His trademark colour became known as Majorelle blue, a strong shade of cobalt that he used for his studio and for the structures holding the garden's various water features.

Equally, Majorelle was in advance of Roberto Burle Marx (see pages 146–48) with his exotic planting, reminiscent of an Henri Rousseau painting and dense enough to conceal any number of tigers. Majorelle not only covered every space

with lush vegetation, but also chose plants for maximum colour impact. The pink walls and columns are hung with magenta bougainvillea and fuchsias, and pelargoniums flourish in those yellow pots. Even the fish in the water tank are a brilliant orange–scarlet. The rest of the planting includes totem-pole and pincushion cacti, palmettos and palms, including the Fiji island palm (*Pritchardia pacifica*), along with bananas, agaves and aloes, bamboos and dragon trees (*Dracaena draco*). Madison Cox, in his book *Artists' Gardens* (1993), describes the atmosphere as secret and enigmatic, one of 'extreme luxuriance and privilege' but also forbidding in the rampage of its vegetation. The effect is unforgettable.

Majorelle's work still exists in all its glory, thanks to eight gardeners who tend this riotous plot. Credit is also due to the couturier Yves St Laurent and his partner, Pierre Bergé, who rescued the garden from near-dereliction after Majorelle's death.

El Generalife
Granada, Spain

El Generalife, built in the early fourteenth
century on the slopes beside the Alhambra
palace in Granada, Spain, is one of the most
famous gardens in the world and, probably,
the one that springs first to many minds
when describing Islamic garden design.
Yet much of the garden and its purpose
are still a mystery, a mystery increased by
a serious fire there in 1958, after which
discoveries were made proving that the
garden we see today is very different from
the one the Nasrid rulers would have
known in the early 1300s.

The name comes from the Arabic,
Jenna-al-arif, which means 'Garden of
the Architect'. However, this garden was
almost certainly not designed by the
architect for himself but created for the
sultans of Granada as a place of relaxation
from the ceremonial gardens of the
official palace. The atmospheres of the
two are very different, with El Generalife
providing privacy and seclusion; its design
speaks of simplicity, elegance and ease.
The garden of El Generalife was probably
adjacent to two other palaces, although,
when the Venetian ambassador Andrea
Navagero visited Granada in 1524 (only
a generation after the last sultan was

Discoveries made at the garden of El Generalife after
a fire in the 1950s have raised more questions about
its original design and use.

ousted), these palaces were already derelict. El Generalife's garden, however, he described as magnificent. At the time, the Alhambra and El Generalife were probably surrounded by orchards and wilderness where wild animals would be hunted.

The main garden consists of a long, narrow canal within a courtyard, the Patio de la Acequia. This is surrounded by cypress and citrus trees underplanted with flowers, and from the surrounding paving fountain jets send skeins of water into the canal. The whole purpose is to create coolness, through the sight, sound and refreshing effect of running water. Research during the restoration in the

1950s, however, showed that these fountains were not original. The early garden had two canals, a long north–south one and a shorter one running east–west. Each was aligned with a *mirador* or belvedere at either end (today only two remain, one at the north, the other at the west). It has also been discovered that in the fourteenth century the flower beds were much lower than the paving, allowing the flowers to give an effect like an oriental carpet. Originally, too, in the western *mirador* there was a large pool, which was used for irrigation and linked to a central fountain at the point where the two canals intersected.

Navagero said there were jets that could be turned on and off with taps to drench the unwary. The Italian Renaissance *giochi d'acqua* (water jokes) may have been inspired by these (see pages 59–61). There was also a water staircase on the eastern side of the garden; the staircase survives, and one can still see the runnels and fountain basins.

El Generalife is poised between the Alhambra above it and the city of Granada, clearly visible below. Outside the main courtyard to the south there are more gardens with pools and fountains. These, however, were created after World War II by Francisco Prieto-Moreno.

Above, left Additions were made to the main garden by Francisco Prieto-Moreno after World War II.

Above, right The common lineage in gardens from India to Spain is unmistakable.

Right The shape of this secluded pool is familiar from Islamic wall-tile patterns. Each lobe of the pool has its own fountain.

Opposite The main Generalife garden contains all the classic elements of an Islamic garden: long, rectangular pools bounded by rectangular beds, cooling jets and an enclosing wall, the planting subservient to geometry.

THE FORMAL WATER GARDEN

When the Renaissance, starting in Italy in the fifteenth century, set Europe free from the stifling clericalism of the medieval period, its architects and artists went back to the Classical principles of ancient Greece and Rome. And, because most garden designers of the Renaissance were actually architects, garden design underwent the same vast change.

As the twentieth-century garden designer (and architect) Sir Geoffrey Jellicoe explained: 'The saga of the Italian garden is richer and more varied than any other garden culture, falling roughly into three periods: the True Renaissance (1400–1500); the High Renaissance (1500–1600) and Mannerism and Baroque (1600–1700) … it was in Rome that the first serious studies were made of the ruins of antiquity and the startling discovery of proportion as an echo of the rational human mind' (*The Landscape of Civilization*, 1989). He then conjures up the formal Renaissance garden: '… the mythological caryatids, the long shady airy arcade, the tremendous folly, the splendid carpet patterned in evergreens and fountains, the music and sparkle of rising and falling waters and the dignity and grandeur of it all'.

The gardens designed by such architects as Bernardo Buontalenti in the sixteenth century and André Le Nôtre in the seventeenth were symmetrical, formal, carefully proportioned and treated like rooms in a palace. Plants played second fiddle to statuary, garden buildings and, most importantly, water.

Water had, of course, been a feature of the gardens of Roman villas, and the canals, fountains and pools that embellished the surroundings of the villas of imperial grandees were fed by miles of aqueducts and complex hydraulic engineering (read Robert Harris's depiction of them in *Pompeii*, 2003). With the Renaissance all this returned, with a lot of showing off. Gilded statues of river

The gardens of the Villa Reale or Pecci-Blunt, near Lucca in Tuscany, include a *teatro d'acqua*, 'Spanish' gardens in the Islamic style and this formal lemon garden.

gods sat above pools, fountains spouted from mythical creatures and watercourses were no longer simple canals but jaw-dropping multiple cascades. Dolphins prance along the gentle cascade at the High Renaissance garden of Palazzo Farnese in Rome, made in 1587, and Pirro Ligorio's double terrace at the Villa d'Este consists of no fewer than one hundred fountains (see pages 59–61).

All this exuberance, however, was required to obey the prevailing rules of architecture. Lines were straight, vistas carefully controlled, asymmetry avoided. At the Medici villa at Pratolino, just north of Florence, however, Buontalenti edged the garden with a necklace of curving pools, each different, which flow into one another as the land descends. Here, in striving for a natural effect (though in a formal manner), he was in advance of his time.

Another manifestation of 'formalized nature' popularized in the Renaissance was the grotto. William Beckford, on his Grand Tour in 1780, delighted in what he encountered at Florence's Boboli Gardens, which Buontalenti had designed for the Medicis.

I found a spring under a rustic arch of grotto work fringed round with ivy. Millions of fish inhabit here, of that beautiful glittering species which comes from China. This golden nation were leaping after insects as I stood gazing upon the deep clear water, and listening to the drops that trickle from the cove. Opposite to which, at the end of an alley of vines, you discover an oval bason [sic] and, in the midst of it a statue of Ganymede, sitting reclined upon the

eagle, full of that graceful languor so peculiarly Grecian. Whilst I was musing on the margin of the spring the moon rose above the tufted foliage of the terraces. (Elizabeth Mavor, *The Grand Tour of William Beckford*, 1986)

A seventeenth-century Venetian senator, Zuane Francesco Barbarigo, was an amateur but enthusiastic garden planner, and for his Villa Barbarigo, near Padua, he designed canals, cascades and rocky outcrops set against the romantic background of the Euganean hills (which Beckford also visited). This mingling of nature with formality was intended to represent the Garden of Eden.

Perhaps the epitome of the Italian Baroque cascade was created by Luigi Vanvitelli and his son Carlo at the Palazzo Reale in Caserta, Campania, where the Bourbon Charles III sought to outdo Versailles. Here, water is brought via canals and aqueducts from 40 kilometres (25 miles) away to feed a cascade that drops 78 metres (225 feet) and then flows 3 kilometres (2 miles) towards the palace through a series of canals and waterfalls. Classical figures – Diana and Actaeon, Venus and Adonis – caught in creamy white Carrara marble disport themselves among the pools and falls.

French gardens were highly influenced by the Renaissance, and many splendid examples survive or have been restored. Best known is Versailles, where André Le Nôtre created lavish spectacles for the Sun King, Louis XIV. Le Nôtre's first major work was at Vaux le Vicomte, for Louis's feted but ultimately ill-fated finance minister, Nicolas Fouquet. The chateau is surrounded by a square moat, the magnificent staircase leading to the front door being the only access to the building. Le Nôtre used the same technique at Chantilly, where the moat is echoed in the outer garden by a large formal lake. These sheets of water have a lightening mirror effect. Indeed, the seventeenth-century French gardens have a lightness of touch that the earlier Italian ones do not.

While Britain also embraced the Classical formality of European gardens – the grand cascade at Chatsworth, in Derbyshire, by Le Nôtre's pupil Grillet, is a stunning survival – when landscaped parkland became all the rage, formal, architectural gardens were suddenly unfashionable and many were dug up, to be lost forever. In the nineteenth century Victorian formality focused on plants rather than water, but there was a revival of interest in the twentieth century, not least from Sir Geoffrey Jellicoe. His gardens at Shute House (see pages 151–53) and at Sutton Place, Surrey, make use of all the Renaissance tricks and skills; indeed, Sutton Place has been described by garden writer Tom Turner as 'the last major English garden to be designed in the Italian style'. When he was eighty-seven Jellicoe designed (though never made) the Moody Historical Gardens on semi-tropical salt marshes at Galveston, Texas, a series of gardens representing historical styles including Roman, Italian Renaissance and French Baroque.

The interest in grand water features has, if anything, grown since the 1990s. The restyling of the garden of Alnwick Castle, Northumberland, included a celebrated series of cascades and fountains, and at Holker Hall in Cumbria a water staircase in the Classical tradition with a central fountain was made in the 1980s. Holker Hall's owner, Lord Cavendish of Furness, argues strongly against mothballing such places: 'I have not the smallest doubt that if we stopped … developing it, [public] interest would quickly tail off.' After all, if gardens, even great gardens, were protected by prohibition, we would not have Pratolino or Versailles to admire.

Opposite André Le Nôtre, designer of the gardens of Versailles, earlier worked at Vaux le Vicomte for France's finance minister, Nicolas Fouquet.

Below, left Designers throughout Europe played with watery themes and some, like this seventeenth-century German example, were extremely fanciful.

Below, right After a long time out of fashion, water staircases are experiencing a revival: this one at Holker Hall, in Cumbria, was constructed in the 1980s.

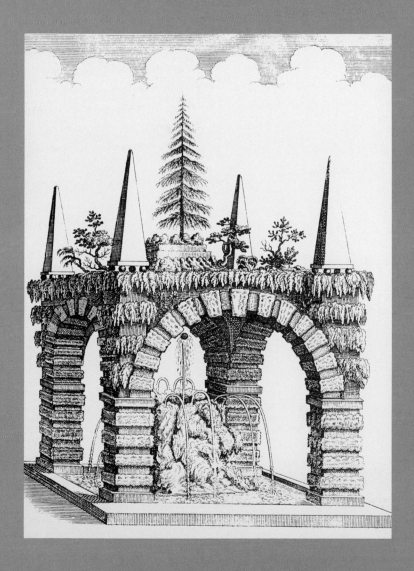

Peterhof
Gulf of Finland, Russia

Like many gardens created in the early eighteenth century, Peterhof is allegorical and political. Its very position is deliberately designed to celebrate Russia's victory over Sweden at the Battle of Poltava in 1709. This victory gave Russia much-needed access to the Baltic Sea, and the reigning tsar, Peter I (reigned 1682–1725), sited Peterhof Palace and its 120 hectares (297 acres) of garden overlooking the Gulf of Finland as a mark of victory.

Like many an absolute monarch, Peter the Great also had a hand in designing the palace and garden. Dmitry Shvidkovsky, professor at the Architectural Institute in Moscow, says that the prolific nineteenth-century horticultural writer J.C. Loudon was inaccurate in claiming that Russia had no gardens before the 1720s (St Petersburg at that time grew more pineapples than the rest of Europe put together, and the Kremlin had hanging gardens with watermelons in the late seventeenth century, for instance). He does, however, concede that Peter the Great's visit to Versailles in 1716 was a turning point in Russian garden design and that Peterhof, as a result, was a conscious mixture of the formal Dutch, French and Italian styles.

Peter the Great created Peterhof's garden to celebrate his victory over Sweden at Poltava.

Peterhof's architect was J.F. Braunstein, but the major work was done by Alexandre Le Blond between 1716 and his death in 1719. After that designers included Niccolò Michetti, who designed many of the fountains, pavilions and cascades, and Bartolomeo Francesco Rastrelli, who worked during the reign of Empress Elizabeth (1741–62). The other great shaper of the Peterhof garden was Catherine the Great, influenced by the gardens of her fellow countryman Frederick II of Prussia at Sans Souci, Potsdam, and by the English landscape movement, as a result of which she employed James Meader of Syon House, London.

Water makes an impressive statement at Peterhof. There are in all three cascades and more than 150 fountains. The water,

brought from a source 22 kilometres (14 miles) away by the engineer Vassily Tuvulkov, flows under the palace and emerges to tumble down a double marble cascade into the Samson basin (the Poltava victory was on St Samson's Day) before flowing out into the sea.

It may be the lack of Versailles vainglory or the competent mixture of Italian, French and Northern European styles that makes Peterhof so magnificent. But perhaps greater than any of these advantages is the superb site. To stand at the top of the Grand Cascade and see the water glistening over the marble stairs, past the dozens of gilded statues and herms, and down the Marine Canal to the sea makes this Baroque Russian palace and its garden utterly memorable.

Opposite, top and bottom left The garden at Peterhof is not understated or faint-hearted, the multiple golden statues and more than 150 ebullient fountains proclaiming success and jubilation.

Opposite, bottom right Peterhof is all about power. The Russian victory at Poltava on St Samson's Day is celebrated by the Samson Basin, where a gilded Samson wrenches open the jaws of a lion, representing Sweden.

Below At Peterhof fountains come in all styles, from trick water-spouting trees to the Lion Cascade, in which jets shoot up between the 8-metre-tall (26 feet) Ionic pillars. This temple-like structure was blown up in World War II and finally restored in 2000.

THE FORMAL WATER GARDEN

Villa d'Este
Tivoli, Italy

The water garden of the Villa d'Este has been hugely influential for more than four hundred years, and its design and *giochi d'acqua* (water jokes) are still copied. As well as influencing other gardens, however, it was itself inspired by much earlier times, both in subject and in construction.

Pirro Ligorio designed the garden between 1560 and 1575 for Cardinal Ippolito II d'Este. Cardinal d'Este, an antiquarian with papal ambitions, and Ligorio, a painter, archaeologist and architect, were well matched (another garden by Ligorio was the Villa Pia, for Pope Pius IV), and the combination of the two created a garden where water is not a mere feature but the essence of the place.

The garden is arranged in three tiers. The topmost has arching fountains that appear, today, from mossy stones with occasional back-arching sprays of water; the second tier spouts water from more stones; and the third set of fountains appears from lions' heads.

Like many gardens of the Italian Renaissance, this was more than a pleasure garden: it was designed to be full of allegory. One may take, for example, an easy garden path leading to Venus and profane

Pirro Ligorio was heavily influenced by Classical mythology. Here one hundred gushing fountains recall Hercules' cleansing of the Augean stables.

59

Right Pirro Ligorio was also an archaeologist, and he used his knowledge when designing and building cascades and grottoes.

Below, right Diana of Ephesus was the inspiration for this many-breasted fountain.

Opposite The garden of the Villa d'Este was hugely influential, and many of the characteristic sprays, jets and statues were copied in gardens designed centuries later.

love, or a steep and rocky route to the goddess Diana and chastity. There is a maze inspired by the Minotaur's Labyrinth in Classical mythology and, a central feature of the garden, the Terrace of One Hundred Fountains, a reference to Hercules' cleansing of the Augean stables. When he visited in 1645, the gardener and diarist John Evelyn commented that the walk of one hundred fountains was 'a long and spacious walk, full of fountains, under which is historiz'd the whole Ovidian metamorphoses in *mezzo rilievo* rarely sculptured'. These sculptures, covered with moss over the centuries and now indistinguishable, originally depicted the forms into which the Olympian gods and goddesses transformed themselves and mortals in Ovid's *Metamorphoses*: Jupiter into a swan, Actaeon into a deer, and so on.

Just as the garden was begun, the University of Padua started a course in water studies, looking at the ancient theories of Archimedes, Aristotle, Vitruvius,

Hero of Alexandria and others. Ligorio's fountain of singing birds at the Villa d'Este was copied from a technique described by Hero, who flourished around the first century AD. Water flowing over flute-like pipes causes the 'birds' to 'sing', but they fall silent at the appearance of a model owl. The seemingly miraculous Organ Fountain, built in 1661, is another feature that drew on first-century hydraulic technology. Time and decay meant that for a long time it was silent, but recent restoration has allowed its music to be heard once more all over the garden.

Since it was created, the garden of the Villa d'Este has been an essential stopping point for tourists and designers, from the seventeenth- and eighteenth-century Grand Tourists onwards. The water jokes, the water organ, the maze and the engineering have been a constant source of inspiration for water gardens on a grand, Classical scale. Franz Liszt even composed a piece in its honour: 'Giochi d'Acqua a Villa d'Este'.

Château d'Annevoie
Namur, Belgium

Should anyone need an example of how
to construct a water garden using solely
gravity and the natural flow of water, the
place to visit is Annevoie. The garden was
created between 1758 and 1775 by a rich
ironmaster, Charles-Alexis de Montpellier,
who inherited the estate in 1750, enlarging
the chateau as well as making the garden.
He was inspired by Versailles and the
Villa d'Este, but, luckily, his fortune was
smaller than that of great kings or dukes,
and the result is less grandiose and more
charming than either.

   Annevoie benefits from a wonderful
natural site. Four springs emerge from
its high point and feed the 400-metre
(1300-foot) *Grand Canal*, which acts as
a reservoir for all the delights below it.
First among these is a charming and very
unusual feature called the *Buffet d'Eau*, a
grassy bank through which balloons of
water bubble up as though by magic, to
flow into the River Rouillon, which itself
provides a natural contrast to the other
contrived waterworks.

   On the other side of the river, nearer
the chateau, is the *Petit Canal* with its
various fountains, all gravity-fed, and
Le Miroir d'Eau, a beautiful still pond

The garden at Annevoie is the creation of an
eighteenth-century ironmaster, and it is a delightful
mixture of the formal and informal.

63

that laps one side of the chateau, reflecting its stone walls.

Part of the fascination of the way water is used at Annevoie is its variety. There are two contrasting waterfalls, the English and the French, a pool called *L'Artichaud* because it is shaped like an artichoke, and the *Fontaine d'Amour*,

where a slight touch on a rock will make the water disappear and where visitors can make a wish. The *Rocher de Neptune* is a fern-clad grotto with a figure of the god sitting beside one of the springs. He is made of iron, as are the *trompe l'oeil* busts of Roman emperors – a reminder of Charles-Alexis's origins. As Barbara Abbs,

author of *Gardens of the Netherlands and Belgium* (1999), writes, the garden shows 'Charles-Alexis de Montpellier's artistry with water ... water glides over a three-tiered cascade. Each level has a scalloped lip. The water falls in an enchanting pattern, noiselessly because of a dip in the ledge below, and then to the next scalloped edge ... . In some places the water glides over curved edges like silver satin, in others it is mirror-still while elsewhere it chatters and glitters.'

The fountains are various, too. Some shoot 6 metres (20 feet) into the air in an arrogant display, like those made so popular by Le Nôtre; others plume out into plashing peacock's tails or bubble quietly from still surfaces. The jets' lead nozzles are often original and need careful cleaning and adjusting to keep the display in trim.

The springs at Annevoie are now protected (as is the garden) to ensure that nothing disturbs the equilibrium of the plan or the purity of the water.

Opposite, top A *buffet d'eau* is usually described as a series of spouts or fountains coming out of a wall, but at Annevoie the basis of the *buffet* is a ripple of grassy terraces.

Opposite, bottom Peacock-tail fountains are an important feature of the garden. The fountains' lead nozzles are carefully maintained originals.

Right and below The garden's fountains and cascades rely entirely on gravity. The upper canal supplies the whole system and the pressure allows some fountains to reach up to 6 metres (20 feet).

LANDSCAPE GARDENS WITH WATER

The first seeds of the inspiration that would result in the great eighteenth-century English landscape garden were sown in the late seventeenth century. Here is John Worlidge, a country gentleman, writing in *The Art of Gardening* in 1683: 'But if the Place you live in be so dry,/ That neither Springs nor Rivers they are nigh,/ Then at some distance from your garden make,/ Within the gaping Earth a spacious lake.'

Around this time, in the mid-seventeenth century, three great painters were creating notional landscapes for their Classical allegories: Salvator Rosa, Gaspard Poussin and Claude Lorrain. William Kent (1685–1748), architect and great garden designer, saw their work on a visit to Rome in 1716, and understood how nature itself could be a source of inspiration, and that naturalistic landscapes could be created within the confines of a garden. As Horace Walpole described in his *Essay on Modern Gardening*, 1785:

> At that moment appeared Kent, painter enough to taste the charms of landscape, bold and opinionated enough to dare and to dictate. He ... saw that all nature was a garden. ... of all the beauties that he added to the face of this beautiful country, none surpassed his management of water. Adieu to canals, circular basons [*sic*] and cascades tumbling down marble steps, the last absurd magnificence of Italian and French villas ... . The gentle stream was taught to serpentine seemingly at its pleasure ... . The living landscape was chastened and polished, not transformed.

Several characteristics of the landscape style emerged: flowing lines to replace the angular symmetry of the formal style it

Idealized scenes in such paintings as this, *Mountain Landscape with Figures and a Man Bathing* by Salvator Rosa (1615–1673), inspired the landscape-garden movement.

usurped; the idea of the 'borrowed view', incorporating the surrounding countryside into contrived 'natural' vistas (something that Chinese and Japanese garden creators had long understood); and – a further inspiration from the 'Arcadian' paintings of Poussin and others – the Classical folly or romantic ruin.

Probably the first recognizable landscape garden was made in 1715 at Studley Royal in Yorkshire (below), where a disgraced Chancellor of the Exchequer, John Aislabie, had rusticated himself from London after being freed from imprisonment in the Tower of London. He had the hills planted with native trees and, while the water was still contained within formal boundaries, the perfect circle and crescents of the Moon Ponds lapped at grass, not stone.

Although Kent, Humphry Repton (1752–1818) and Lancelot 'Capability' Brown (1716–1783) are considered the great landscape designers of the period, some of the best landscape gardens were made by amateurs, the poet William Shenstone among them. Taking over his family home and farm, The Leasowes in England's West Midlands, in 1743, Shenstone spent the next two decades refashioning it as a *ferme ornée*, creating winding walks through the woodlands and adding naturalistic planting, pools and waterfalls. He is thought to be the first to call himself a 'landscape gardener'.

Shenstone also worked with the banker Henry Hoare, whose estate at Stourhead is one of the greatest examples of a landscape

garden (see pages 75–77). Painshill Park, in Surrey, was the work of another amateur, the Hon. Charles Hamilton. He brought water up from the River Mole to form a long, large lake, and excelled in the folly stakes: along with the near-obligatory Gothick ruin and Classical temple, Painshill has a triumphal arch, a 'Chinese' bridge, a 'Turkish tent' and, of course, a grotto. One of the most magnificent grottoes was that created at Goldney Hall, near Bristol: three large chambers encrusted with shellwork carried out by the owner's daughters (references to the sea and to river gods were a frequent feature, as was dripping water).

Not all landscape garden designers were of the same mind. William Chambers's dislike of the more successful Brown made him insist that the landscape movement was inspired by Chinese mountain and lake gardens (he, unlike Brown, had visited China), while Charles Bridgeman, probable inventor of the haha and disdainer of symmetry, was countered by Batty Langley: 'The same extravagant way of thinking prevailed also to a great degree … in his Plan of Lakes and Pieces of Water, without any regard to the Goodness of the Land, which was to be overflowed. But which he generally designed so large, as to make a whole Country look like an Ocean' (*New Principles of Gardening*, 1728).

A fair point, but what was a landscape garden without lakes, streams and rivers? And the water had to be, in Shenstone's words, 'the waving line', not the rigid symmetry of the formal style. By the mid-eighteenth century water had taken over as the main feature in the landscape. 'Water is the most interesting object in a landscape,' said the politician and garden writer Thomas Whately in his *Observations on Modern Gardening* (1770). '[It] captivates the eye at a distance, invites approach, and is delightful when near; … in form, in style, and in extent, [it] may be made equal to the greatest compositions or adapted to the least: it may spread in a calm expanse to sooth[e] the tranquillity of a peaceful scene; or hurrying along a devious course, add splendor [*sic*] to a gay, and extravagance to a romantic, situation.' This, as Laurence Fleming and Alan Gore write in *The English Garden* (1980), 'sums up the attitude in the 1760s to water, [which was] about to become an essential ingredient in every park in England'.

Despite its French and Italian artistic origins, the landscape style is seen as quintessentially English. That is not to say,

Left The circular pool and flanking crescent moons at Studley Royal maintain a formal symmetry, but the temple and the absence of flower beds or formal planting indicate a move towards the landscape style.

Opposite, top Paintings of pastoral landscapes with rivers, lakes and temples and, in Claude's *Landscape with Apollo and Muses*, lounging gods, were a source of inspiration to eighteenth-century garden designers.

Opposite, bottom West Wycombe Park in Buckinghamshire, with its Temple of Music reflected in the lake, typifies the English landscape garden.

however, that it was limited to British shores. The landscape passion spread throughout Europe, even on land too hilly, too flat or too drought-ridden to support it successfully. The Russian aristocracy, in particular, embraced the idea of the 'English park' with a passion. Catherine the Great employed John Busch, a Hackney nurseryman, to create a landscape garden at her favourite country residence, Tsarskoe Selo, and her lover, Prince Potemkin, used William Gould from Lancashire (known as the 'Capability' Brown of Russia) for his park at the Tauride Palace in St Petersburg. Charles Cameron designed the garden at nearby Pavlovsk for Grand Duke Paul, and the duke's wife, Maria Fedorovna, later took on Busch to make another landscape garden at Gatchina.

The landscape style has been suggested by many to be England's greatest contribution to garden design. I disagree, because it entailed the disastrous razing of wonderful seventeenth-century gardens. For this reason I see 'Capability' Brown as a villain rather than a hero. During his working lifetime he 'improved' nearly a hundred gardens, from Alnwick Castle in Northumberland to Wycombe Abbey in Buckinghamshire (although Repton was responsible for even more). The landscaping fashion would sweep away such fine seventeenth-century gardens as that at Blenheim Palace in Oxfordshire, where Brown also enlarged the lake and did away with the Vauban-inspired bastions at the front of the house. Fleming and Gore also disapprove: 'Of all [his] alterations to the gardens of his predecessors, few were more disastrous than his destruction of the garden at Blenheim. The vast palace now sits on a lawn which, visually, does not support its weight.'

Indeed, it is worth remembering, when one sees a William and Mary, Queen Anne or early Georgian house surrounded by parkland, that such a setting was never intended. Such palatial blocks as Blenheim or plainer manor houses were not supposed to be in landscapes, and they are often not happy there, looking somehow divorced from their surroundings. However, the landscape park, being easier to maintain than the intensely gardened earlier style with its canals, topiary, *allées* and parterres, has had a better survival rate than the formal garden, and many still exist, at least in part. They were designed for posterity, and posterity is now enjoying them.

Schloss Wörlitz
Sachsen-Anhalt, Germany

The citation conferring UNESCO World
Heritage Site status on the gardens of
Schloss Wörlitz and the *Gartenreich*
or 'garden kingdom' says they are 'an
outstanding example of the application
of the philosophical principles of the
Age of Enlightenment', integrating 'arts,
education and economy in a harmonious
whole'. These gardens certainly
deserve such superlatives, for they are
extraordinary. The estate of Schloss
Wörlitz, near Halle in what was East
Germany, had by the end of the
Communist era all but vanished under
vast stretches of *Rhododendron
ponticum*. The greatest landscape garden
in central Europe was almost lost.

The gardens were the creation of
Prince Leopold III Friedrich Franz von
Anhalt-Dessau between 1765 and 1817,
following his numerous travels around
English landscape gardens, often with no
fewer than three gardeners in tow. He was
especially influenced by Stourhead (see
pages 75–77), Claremont (see pages 79–81)
and Stowe, and his Temple of Venus was a
copy of Colen Campbell's temple at Hall
Barn, Buckinghamshire.

The prince did not confine himself
to a single park, but incorporated farms,

The *Gartenreich* contains palaces, farm buildings and
the church and synagogue at Oranienbaum.

estates and no fewer than six palaces into his design. Today his *Gartenreich* is only a quarter of its original size, but nonetheless stretches for some 25 kilometres (15 miles) along the bank of the River Elbe and its tributaries. Water is a constant presence, enjoyed as lakes and water meadows, or on boat trips on meandering rivers. At Wörlitz itself there are nineteen bridges but no fences, and when the park was later reworked after floods in 1770, lakes were sensibly created where the flood water had gathered. An *Île des Peupliers* ('island of poplars') pays tribute to Jean-Jacques Rousseau with a copy of the writer's tomb at Ermenonville, and elsewhere there is a lake in the manner of 'Capability' Brown with two islands. A pastiche of an Italian landscape is complete with

Pantheon, Italian peasant's house and, perched on a rocky island outcrop called the Stein, the Villa Hamilton, dedicated to Sir William Hamilton (rather than his wife and Nelson's mistress, Lady Hamilton), the great collector and vulcanologist, with whom Prince Leopold toured Italy. The rocks include watery grottoes and a Vesuvius that could be made to spit fire.

Everywhere there are references to the English style that the prince so admired. At Oranienbaum, the palace in the south-eastern part of the *Gartenreich*, a park in the Anglo-Chinese style boasts canals, tea houses and a pagoda inspired by Sir William Chambers's at Kew (see page 21), while the grounds around the Luisium Palace have a large lake with a Palladian bridge, a well and a grotto.

The English landscape style may have inspired this monumental feat, but nothing in England compares with the size and ambition of Wörlitz and its realm.

Above Boats are moored outside the sixteenth-century Schloss Kirche. This palace was intended to be seen from the water.

Opposite, top left These huge gardens have no fewer than nineteen bridges in various styles crossing the meandering streams. This meadow is a mass of mauve crocuses in the spring.

Opposite, right, top to bottom Classical statues were carefully positioned as eye-catchers and to instil a pensive mood; the buildings included not only temples but also mills, a *Chinesisches Haus* ('Chinese house', seen here) and farm buildings in the *cottage orné* style; this tiny island pays homage to Jean-Jacques Rousseau.

Opposite, bottom left At 120 hectares (296 acres), this is a water garden on a truly enormous scale.

Stourhead
Wiltshire, England

It is curious and sad that the garden at Stourhead, which George Plumptre calls 'one of the most complete statements of the landscape movement ... the complete realization of one man's vision of landscape' (*The Garden Makers*, 1993), should have been conceived as a result of tragedy.

The 'one man' was banker Henry Hoare (1705–1785), grandson of the man who founded Hoare's Bank of London; the tragedy was that it was mourning that plunged him into garden design. He started to create the garden when his first wife died after only a year of marriage, and he continued in 1743 following the premature death of his second wife after fifteen years of marriage.

Hoare was a cultivated man and lover of Classical art and architecture, so when he looked for some diversion from his sorrow, he took to gardening, inspired by the landscapes of the painter Claude Lorrain. The two pictures that were especially influential were *Imaginary View of Delphi with a Procession* (Hoare owned a copy by Andrea Locatelli) and *Coast View of Delos with Aeneas*. The Doric portico in the former inspired

Stourhead, the epitome of the landscape garden, was in fact designed by an amateur, the banker Henry Hoare.

75

Stourhead's Temple of Flora, and the Pantheon and bridge in the latter were models for Stourhead's miniature Pantheon, with its statue of Hercules, and the five-arched bridge over the lake. What brings Stourhead firmly into the English landscape is the backdrop of the parish church of Stourton and glimpses of the village. 'The bridge, village and church altogether will be a charming Gaspard [i.e. the artist, Poussin] picture at the end of the water', commented Hoare in a letter to a friend.

The garden at Stourhead began with its outstanding feature: an 8-hectare (20-acre) lake, which Hoare created by damming the source of the River Stour on his land. This is central to the whole garden, which should be seen by making a circuit of the lake, a promenade that reveals the vistas and buildings from many angles. Suggestions that this was conceived as an allegory of the journey in Virgil's *Aeneid* have now been dismissed as no more than incidental, but there is certainly the sense that a tour of the garden is also a journey.

Like all good bankers and rich garden creators, Henry Hoare gathered a studio of artists and architects around him. The house, hardly visible, was designed by Colen Campbell for Hoare's father in 1722, and Hoare commissioned Henry Flitcroft as his resident architect, knowing that Flitcroft had worked with designers Lord Burlington and William Kent. Flitcroft's work includes the various temples and bridges, while the Classical statues that decorate the garden are by John Cheere and Michael Rysbrack. Rysbrack's work includes the statue of Hercules in the Pantheon (formerly the Temple of Hercules), and Cheere designed the sleeping *Nymph of the Grot*. She lies in a grotto with water gushing beneath her, a river god's urn (also pouring with water) beside her, the picturesque scene lit by a hole in the ceiling.

When Henry Hoare died in 1785, his nephew, Richard Colt Hoare, inherited the estate. He planted ornamental trees around Stourhead, as did a later Sir Henry, in 1894. Purists still grumble that these later changes spoil the purity of the landscape. In 1946 Stourhead passed to the National Trust.

Opposite and above, left The garden encourages the idea that the visitor is taking a journey through a Classical landscape. The central lake covers 8 hectares (20 acres) and is fed by the River Stour, which Henry Hoare dammed.

Above, right A bearded river god sits within a darkened watery grotto. Circular holes in the roof of the grotto allow in enough daylight for visitors to see their way in the gloom, and provide an effective form of natural spotlighting.

Claremont
Surrey, England

If any garden epitomizes the rise and change of the English landscape garden, it is that of Claremont in Surrey. This unusual garden is to be treasured for having had so many of the great artists of the landscape movement work on it. Sir John Vanbrugh, architect of Blenheim and Castle Howard among many other great houses, bought the estate in 1708 because of 'the situation being singularly Romantick'. But he smartly sold it on (in 1714) to Sir Thomas Pelham-Holles, who subsequently became Duke of Newcastle and twice served as prime minister.

Vanbrugh, who had built the house and created a belvedere in the garden, continued to carry out work on the estate for the duke. By 1716 his colleague and collaborator, Charles Bridgeman, had arrived to help create the house's surroundings. Bridgeman was an interesting garden designer, for he was responsible for the change in style from seventeenth-century formal to eighteenth-century landscape. This transitional work can still be seen at Claremont.

Bridgeman's most exciting contribution to the garden was a great turf amphitheatre, copied from the

The garden at Claremont is significant because it is transitional in style between seventeenth-century formality and eighteenth-century landscaping.

Classical model. It consisted of four semicircular concave terraces descending to a central lookout point, below which four convex terraces fanned out to form the full circle. Further down the sloping site was a formal round pond with an island reached over a chinoiserie bridge. Beyond the pond the design showed elements of landscape-style parkland.

All this is known from a surviving picture that illustrates these features in great detail (above), but by 1729 William Kent had been called in to create further features – notably a serpentine haha – and either he or Bridgeman remodelled the round pool into a naturalistic lake, following the new fashion. The island was given a pavilion designed by Kent, called the New House, and the south bank of the new lake gained a cascade, formed using a natural stream. In the 1760s more

changes were made: the cascade was transformed into an enormous rustic grotto, possibly by Josiah and Joseph Lane, who were working on the garden of Painshill nearby.

When the duke died, in 1768, the whole estate was bought by Lord Clive, who brought in 'Capability' Brown. Brown rebuilt Vanbrugh's house and covered the Bridgeman amphitheatre with trees.

The National Trust took on Claremont's garden in 1949 and (wisely, in my view) decided to remove Brown's trees. In 1975 the Trust reinstated Bridgeman's amphitheatre, so today visitors can see a range of styles: the amphitheatre, Kent's pavilion on the island and the serpentine lake, Vanbrugh's belvedere on a distant hill and the rustic grotto. This is a remarkable survival, especially of Bridgeman's work, of which little has lasted.

Above An early painting gives a bird's-eye view of Bridgeman's complex amphitheatre beside a lake with an island.

Opposite In the eighteenth century 'Capability' Brown planted trees over Bridgeman's design, but the National Trust, which now owns the garden, has removed Brown's planting on the amphitheatre and restored it to Bridgeman's design.

THE ROMANTIC WATER GARDEN

If formal garden style was about firm control and landscape style about secret control, the romantic garden metaphorically lets loose its stays and enjoys nature without too much interference – although, of course, interference there is. It is like managed forestry: the effect appears completely natural but anything that offends the eye – the wrong sort of weed, the badly shaped tree, the muddy stream – is improved or removed. The description 'picturesque', used by garden designers from the late eighteenth century onwards, is an appropriate one: the intention was to create a scene that could have come from a painting, but not one of those eighteenth-century portraits of aristocratic landowners posing in their formal parkland. The Romantics hated Lancelot 'Capability' Brown and his parks with a passion. Sir Uvedale Price, in his *Essays on the Picturesque* (1794–1801), suggested that Brown thought himself mightier than the painter Claude Lorrain (a heresy at the time): 'That such a man [Brown], full of enthusiasm for this new art … should chuse to shew the world what Claude might have been, had he had the advantage of seeing the works of Mr. Brown.'

William Gilpin, a fervent champion of the picturesque in gardening, was also critical (in *Observations on Various Parts of Britain and an Influential Book of Remarks on Forest Scenery*, 1791):

If there be a natural river, or a real ruin in the scene … the best use be made of it: but I should be cautious in advising the creation of either … Mr Brown, I think, has failed more in river-making than in any of his attempts. An artificial lake has sometimes a good effect; but neither propriety, nor beauty can arise from it unless the heads and the extremities of it are perfectly well managed and concealed: and, after all, the success is hazardous.

Artists in different eras have strongly influenced garden styles. Claude Monet's paintings of water lilies sparked new interest in romantic, informal water gardens.

The bridge is a much more basic, rustic structure and the house romantically turreted rather than imposingly Palladian in style. The picturesque, wrote Knight, was inspired by such painters as Titian and Gainsborough. Brown's landscapes were sterile and prim, lacking in subtlety, 'dull, vapid, smooth'. A Brown landscape

> bade the steam 'twixt banks close shaven glide;
> Banish'd the thickets of high-bow'ring wood,
> Which hung, reflected, o'er the glassy flood;
> Where screen'd and shelter'd from the heats of day,
> Oft on the moss-grown stone repos'd I lay,
> And tranquil view'd the limpid stream below,
> Brown with o'erhanging shade, in circling eddies flow.

Other artists, painting in the nineteenth century, defined the picturesque for a generation of gardeners. Very seductive, if out of character, is John Atkinson Grimshaw's *A Mossy Glen* (1864), full of twining ivy, ferns and mossy boulders. James Guthrie's *Hard At It* (opposite) is entirely different in style, but romanticizes the landscape artist, hard at work in an idealized setting.

Although historically the Romantic movement of garden design grew directly out of the landscape style and, like it, drew inspiration from the Grand Tour and the artistic vision of poets and painters, this chapter is more about romance as we see it today when describing scenery: something beautiful and mysterious. John Keats, a true Romantic poet, sums this up in his 'Ode to a Nightingale' when he writes of gardens with 'fast fading violets cover'd up in leaves' and 'the coming musk-rose filled with dewy wine', of 'Charm'd magic casements, opening on the foam/ Of perilous seas, in faery lands forlorn.'

Romantic water gardens have an intangible essence rather than a definable style, and the three in this chapter are all very different creations. I decided to include Columbine Hall here, for example,

The Romantic water garden therefore aimed by a tweak here and a vista there to show how supremely beautiful nature could be if left, almost, to herself. It hoped to evoke an indrawn breath, a moment of delight when the sun shines on rippling water and the moon catches a silvery fountain.

A pair of engravings (below) by Thomas Hearne to accompany Richard Payne Knight's poem 'The Landscape: A Didactic Poem' of 1794 neatly illustrates the differences between the 'landscaped' and the 'romantic'. The first (left) shows a park in which an immaculate river winds through manicured green meadows and is crossed by a neat bridge. Perfectly placed in the background is the main house, framed by stands of trees. The second engraving (right) shows the same scene made in the Romantic mould. The trees have become overgrown, their trunks are covered with ivy and some branches have fallen. The neat lawns have become outcrops of rock with ferns and vegetation.

after seeing Peter Baistow's photographs, taken soon after dawn on one of the hottest imaginable June days (see pages 94–97). The smoking, wreathing mist coming up from the moat and the way it made the ordinary somehow enchanted was a revelation.

Many truly romantic gardens have been created by artists for themselves, partly to please their own senses and partly as a working tool. The most famous of these is Monet's garden at Giverny (see pages 91–93), and it was Giverny that led me to include this chapter of water gardens that defy any categorization but romantic. Twentieth-century artist–gardeners have included the Bloomsbury Group, who painted and gardened at various members' houses. Dora Carrington's painting of her own home, *The Mill at Tidmarsh* (*c.* 1920), is the perfect romantic garden setting: a millpond with two swans sailing on it, reeds and trees, and a quaint mill in the background. A similar coterie of artists worked and gardened in Suffolk. Where Cedric Morris gardened at Benton End, Hadleigh, along with Lett Haines and various pupils, including Lucien Freud and Maggi Hambling, he developed both irises and poppies in the colours he loved to paint. Nearby lived two other artist–gardeners, John Nash and John

Aldridge, although they were more concerned with plants, light and colour than with garden design or water features, as have been other artists who have taken flowers as their inspiration, such as Childe Hassam on the New Hampshire island of Appledore, and Elizabeth Blackadder in Scotland.

Romantic water gardens, then, are rarely the work of professional garden designers and frequently the work of artists, whether poets or painters, who pour artistry into the making of a garden and often draw their art from the garden they have made.

Opposite, top Using his own garden as a model, Monet produced series of waterscapes at all times of the day and in all seasons.

Opposite, bottom The poet Richard Payne Knight rebelled against the sterility that 'Capability' Brown imposed, and Thomas Hearne's illustrations for Knight's poem 'The Landscape' contrast the neat artifice of the landscape style with the untamed, more romantic appeal of the same scene apparently left to Mother Nature.

Below James Guthrie's *Hard At It* (1833) depicts a painter at work amid the Romanticized delights of the English seaside.

Ninfa
Latina, Italy

Not many people have the chance to
create a garden from a ruined medieval
town set on a spectacularly steep
mountainside. But we can imagine the
delight of re-creating the town plan with
plants, the tremendous opportunities
given by hundreds of old stone buildings,
now ruined and roofless, and the challenge
of creating new bridges leaping the
tumbling streams that rush down from
the old wells and watering places.

For the Caetani family, this most
romantic of garden sites was not a
daydream but reality. Ninfa, near Rome,
belonged to them even before the
town was sacked in 1382 as a result of
opposition to the pope of the day. In its
heyday Ninfa was a sizeable community,
boasting a cathedral and seven churches,
but all was lost when it was laid waste
by papal decree, and it lay deserted for
six hundred years.

In the twentieth century, however, the
Caetani family repossessed the derelict
town with the intention of creating a
garden among its streets and ruined
buildings. In the 1920s Duke Gelasio
Caetani began to drain the nearby
marshes, home to swarms of malarial

The wisteria-covered bridge in the wildly romantic
garden of the Caetani family is a clear echo of
Monet's (see pages 91–93).

87

mosquitoes. He made sure that the walls of the old buildings were fully stabilized, and canalized the river that ran through the town. Meanwhile his English mother, the Duchess of Sermoneta, began – as Englishwomen do – to plant quantities of old-fashioned roses against the ancient walls. These loved the climate and the freedom to ramble over the old stones. She also planted cypresses, their sky-rocket shape so typical of the Italian landscape, along the lines of the old streets, to create punctuation marks and emphasize formality and axes. Other Mediterranean trees included the evergreen ilex and black walnuts (*Juglans nigra*) as well as *Magnolia grandiflora*, well suited to the region. A vast reservoir was constructed

to store enough water to keep this luxuriant planting healthy and flourishing.

At first, native Italian trees were favoured, but gradually the old town became home to all manner of exotics. This was the inspiration of Marguerite Chapin, the American wife of Duke Gelasio's brother Roffredo. In the twenty-five years they spent living in the village – the medieval town hall had been restored and made into a home for Duke Gelasio – Roffredo and Marguerite planted a huge range of plants that thrived in the sheltered conditions, including *Drimys winteri* from Chile, *Cladrastis sinensis* from China, hoherias from New Zealand and Montezuma pines from Mexico. They also created more pools and rivulets to

join the streams already flowing into the River Ninfa, which lies at the heart of the garden, adding new watery habitats and further romantic idylls.

Their daughter Lelia, an artist, continued to work on the garden at Ninfa with her husband, Hubert Howard, until her death in 1971. She lined the old pathways with bushes of rosemary, added more old roses and climbers up the walls, as her grandmother had done, and filled streams with white-flowering arum lilies (*Zantedeschia aethiopica*). There are no more members of the family tending the garden today, but the work continues through the Caetani Foundation.

Opposite The hand of the English Duchess of Sermoneta is evident in the unrestrained, informal planting at Ninfa. This smoke tree (*Cotinus coggygria*) creates a particularly beautiful picture when in flower.

Above, left The lushness encouraged by the Italian climate, the pretty streams, the relaxed English style of planting and the ruins of the town combine in wonderful romantic harmony.

Above, right Strong uprights of bamboo and irises – both water-loving – are an effective contrast to the naturalistic pond.

Right Ninfa's ruins are fully exploited, with tumbling climbers and rustic stone bridges adding to the timelessness of the garden.

Giverny
Normandy, France

Picture, if you will, the house and garden of Clos Normande in the village of Giverny in 1882: a plain suburban house, a typically French garden, all disciplined beds. Then picture the scene in 1892, when the painter Claude Monet (1840–1926) has already been gardening there for a decade and decides to buy an extra plot. It is by no means an attractive prospect: unconnected to the house and main garden, it is reached through a tunnel under a railway; its ground is dismally boggy, enlivened only by a few wild irises and native water lilies.

This unpromising spot is, of course, what the artist turned into one of the most famous gardens of the twentieth century and what led to some of the most famous Impressionist paintings: the dozens of water-lily paintings that Monet created during the last three decades of his life. 'I am good for nothing but painting and gardening', he once wrote. But he was very, very good at both.

Experts have often said that Monet's transformation of the garden at Giverny took not the slightest notice of prevailing fashions in gardens. He seemed to be totally unaware of them. Instead, he

Where else could this be but Giverny, Monet's garden in northern France? It has been copied thousands of times but remains inimitable.

planted like the Impressionist he was: beds full of luxurious plants in seductive colours, some controlled in blocks, other areas more variable, where self-seeding plants did the work for him. His gardening palette included lots of *Iris × germanica*, nasturtiums (*Tropaeolum majus*), grape hyacinths (*Muscari* spp.), jonquils, tree peonies, azaleas and rhododendrons.

Roses were caught up in hoops painted a soft teal. All these plants are notable for their colour and their abundance, truly romantic in shape and form.

Monet's water garden is now the most famous in France, if not the world. From that dismal bog beside the railway he created the sort of idyll he saw in the Japanese woodblock prints he collected.

The famous bridge, painted a soft green rather than the traditional lacquer red, is swathed with dripping wisteria, white *W. floribunda* and lilac-flowered *W. sinensis*. Their grey stems twine sinuously from either end and cover the bridge, meeting at its centre. At either end clumps of bamboo stand sentinel.

Among the five gardeners, plus a head gardener, that Monet employed, one was hired to look after the water alone. Its clarity and the disposition of the water lilies and edging irises were important for the paintings as well as the garden. Around the edges of the long pond, a path snakes among the bamboos, gunnera, irises and peonies, creating vistas that seem to be living Impressionist paintings. Like these paintings, the water garden is full of light and sunlight, a visual feast of sensuous flowers and colours, and deeply romantic.

Of course, there have been dissenters. Sir Gerald Kelly, the English painter, was one. 'It was nice and large and covered with rambling crimson roses which, you know, you get practically speaking in any suburban garden all over England. And there was a little piece of water where there were some common or garden water lilies.' Kelly had Monet's gift neither for painting nor for gardening, so maybe he was just jealous.

Left The famous, slightly oriental-looking bridge curves picturesquely over the water, the heavy, coiling stems of its wisteria supported by an overhead frame.

Opposite, top Water lilies are, of course, the signature plant of Giverny, and Monet painted countless series of them during the last decades of his life.

Opposite, bottom left Monet was a painter who thrilled to different seasons and times of day. His romantic vision is always enhanced by early-morning mists

Opposite, bottom right Water lilies, weeping willows and reflections in the water are the essence of Giverny's character.

Columbine Hall
Suffolk, England

If it seems immodest of me to pick my own garden at Columbine Hall, I can say in defence that this was where my interest in water in the garden began. This garden was where we experimented with the advantages of water, how to present it and plant around it, and how to use it in the landscape.

The setting for the medieval jettied house, dating from 1390, has been called romantic for as long as people have been writing about the old manor. The two storeys rise straight from a wide and deep moat – more than 4 metres (14 feet) deep and a good 9 metres (30 feet) wide in most places. The water laps directly against the dining-room and kitchen walls, and commentators have likened the house to a great liner at anchor. Many French manor houses enjoy this same type of aquatic disposition, and the inspiration for both the building and the moat probably came direct from the Normans, as did the name, which originates from that of a Norman lord, Philippe de Columbers.

Tackling the gardens around such an ancient building and moat needed restraint, I felt. While it would have been tempting to cover the steep banks of the

Early-morning mist heralding a hot summer's day wreathes the native trees around Columbine Hall's medieval moat.

moat with, for example, cascades of climbing old-fashioned roses, and to plant them with sheets of yellow daffodils, we prefer to leave them semi-wild. There are areas of scrub and willow (interspersed with red-stemmed willows, *Salix alba* var. *vitellina* 'Britzensis') where the mallard ducks, moorhens and coots can dabble and nest, and there are overhanging branches where the kingfisher perches. The moat is stocked with golden orfe and roach, which, in the summer, swim to the surface, where I'm afraid they fall victim to the kingfisher and the herons.

Little grows in the moat apart from reedmace (*Typha latifolia*, rather striking but not to be encouraged) and, around the borders, wild flag irises, which throw up citrus-yellow flowers in early summer. This limited plant roll call is not for want of trying, but arum lilies and water lilies just don't perform.

In a separate area, with its own intermittent stream, we grow bog plants, which appreciate the moist soil and provide a change of pace from the formality within the moat (much designed by George Carter) to the semi-wild and sinuous without. The water from the moat also provides a spouting Father Thames at its outlet, a series of small ponds designed for their mirror qualities, and a discreet, small waterfall at the head of the bog garden.

Opposite, top The moat, up to 9 metres (30 feet) wide in places, surrounds the manor house and a formal garden of about 0.4 hectares (1 acre).

Opposite, bottom An old farm building beside the moat has been transformed into an eighteenth-century 'eyecatcher'.

Right The house, the remains of something grander and larger, abuts the moat directly on two sides, giving views from the windows across the water to the Suffolk countryside.

Below Cattle grazing in the manor's parkland beyond the moat are caught looking curiously over one of several ornamental bridges.

THE ISLAND WATER GARDEN

There is nothing more romantic than an island, especially one that is small enough to walk round in a day. Islands pack into a tiny space a whole series of different moods and scenery, from mountain to beach, wilderness to manicured garden.

There are some islands – the breathtaking island of Tobago or the eerie, haunting and remote west coast of Lewis, off Scotland, to name just two – where it would be folly to try to improve on nature, but one of the beauties of an island is that the surrounding sea provides an anonymous backdrop, allowing the creation of a world that might be quite divorced from its geographical location.

Every island has its own aura and, luckily for gardeners, its own microclimate. The islands of the Mediterranean benefit from cooling breezes that lessen the summer heat, but these can turn into ferocious winds, so windbreak trees are a familiar feature. Once these are established, each island can create its own garden. On Ischia in the Bay of Naples, Lady Walton, the widow of the composer Sir William, has created a fantastically (and suitably) operatic garden of tropical flowers and greenery, incorporating captivating views of the blue sea from its steeply sloping paths.

The same sea washes the shores of Vulcano, the island off Sicily that gave its name to volcanoes, via the blacksmith god, Vulcan, himself. But here the character is quite different, the beauty sulphurous. There are hot springs and pools and contorted rocks in the waters of bays fringed with fine black sand (the result of past eruptions), and wild, brilliantly coloured flowers with succulent leaves grow where they can. Here, the islanders go with the flow, opting for brightly coloured displays in window boxes and tubs.

On the other side of the world, the gardeners of Dangar Island (left), on the Hawkesbury River near Sydney, have also allowed

On Dangar Island, near Sydney, the residents decided to leave the landscape to nature and encourage birds and wildlife around their houses.

their natural surroundings to take the lead. The island's well-heeled inhabitants have consciously preserved the native bush and wildlife, bringing the flora and fauna to within reach of the houses' windows. There are, luckily, no large animals but wonderful birds. 'Kookaburras, magpies, currawongs and rainbow lorikeets regularly land on the rail and demand to be fed,' says one owner, the architect Terry Dorrough. 'The lorikeets screech like small parrots and are very colourful.' He also loves the changing shadows, patterns and colours that water provides. This is a form of gardening where design, texture and movement are left to nature and colour is added via wildlife rather than plants.

The island environment is not always kind enough to allow gardeners to go with the flow in this way. Around Läckö Slött, a huge Baroque island castle at the edge of Lake Vänern in Sweden, the climate can produce frosts from September to May, allowing only three months for the garden to flourish. But, under the care of the British designer Simon Irvine, flourish it does. Annuals planted each year in different groupings grow phenomenally in the long, light days of the short summer and produce a stunningly colourful display. This is gardening with one hand tied behind your back, but the result is beautiful, if slightly melancholy.

The garden that Gertrude Jekyll constructed on Holy Island, or Lindisfarne, on the north-east coast of England, also gives a sense of battling the elements. The tiny garden is like an island on an island. It lies, seemingly adrift on the windswept rocky moor, a short walk from Lindisfarne's wonderfully stern but romantic fortress, which Sir Edwin Lutyens converted into a theatrical castle. Once within the encircling walls that protect the garden from the fierce North Sea weather, one finds oneself in a little oasis in true Jekyll style: charming, cottagey and very much in the English vernacular tradition.

Despite their northern latitude, the islands off the west coast of Scotland have the benefit of being washed by the friendly, warming Gulf Stream, so that frosts and snow are rare. Relations of my husband's family once owned the Isle of Eigg, in the Inner Hebrides, and they created there a subtropical garden around an Italianate villa, The Lodge. Palm trees lined the drive and, as Camille Dressler recounted in her book of the island, 'around the house a Chilean flame tree, magnolias, strawberry trees, New Zealand daisies and other exotic species gave way to copper beeches, horse chestnut and eucalyptus trees. The warming influence of the Gulf Stream allowed … a wealth of exotic species … . The whole effect was stunning: such a wealth of colours in sharp contrast with the stark moorland a little distance from The Lodge' (*Eigg: The Story of an Island*, 1998). Shelter belts allowed for an apple orchard and drifts of daffodils and narcissi. The garden, she adds, is still an amazing sight, with children playing hide-and-seek among the exotic bushes. In the distance is the rugged Sgurr of Eigg, the island's mountain.

Very different gardens have evolved on other Hebridean islands. On the tiny island of Gigha, for example, Sir James Horlick created at Achamore a habitat in which to grow tender species of rhododendron, along with drifts of Asiatic primulas, camellias and cordylines – Achamore tends more to the Himalayas than Eigg's subtropical paradise. And at An Cala, on the island of Seil, a little further up the coast, the mood is different again. A row of old distillery cottages hugs the cliffs, and the garden's aquatic element comes from a stream, ponds and a waterfall as well as the sea. 'This', says *The Good Gardens Guide*, 'is how azaleas and rhododendrons should be planted on the small scale – enhancing rather than dominating the picture.' The result is charming, even lush, a tiny jewel caught between grey lowering hills and a frequently grey and rough ocean. Every island garden is different.

Opposite, top On Ischia in the Bay of Naples, La Mortella is a suitably operatic garden for the widow of the composer Sir William Walton.

Opposite, bottom Callanish stone circle, on Lewis in the Outer Hebrides, is the antithesis of Ischia, but its remote setting by the Atlantic has its own eerie beauty.

Above, right An Cala, on the Scottish island of Seil, is a cottage garden in a magnificent seaside setting, with great hills behind.

Right The residents of Dangar Island live and garden by the water and go to work by boat.

THE ISLAND WATER GARDEN

Isola Bella
Piedmont, Italy

Isola Bella has certainly not always been a beautiful island: in the sixteenth century it was a bleak, barren rock. Today, however, as you drive along the shores of Lake Maggiore, on the border between Switzerland and Italy, and catch sight of the island just offshore, Isola Bella most surely lives up to its name. It is splendidly generous with its beauty, and looks as spectacular from the mainland as it does from the palace on the island itself.

In 1632 Count Carlo Borromeo, who wanted a summer palace on the island, commissioned Angelo Crivelli as the main architect of palace and garden. After Crivelli's early death, Borromeo and his son Vitaliano continued to embellish this fantastic structure, using Carlo Fontano as architect. The whole was as complete as it was ever to be by the 1690s (it was never entirely finished), a perfect expression of the seventeenth-century Italian Baroque style. It is generally agreed that Isola Bella looks like an extraordinary ship moored on the lake, something between a Venetian doge's *bucintoro* and one of those gigantic gin palaces owned by Russian oligarchs. An early engraving shows that the

A once bleak and barren rock in Lake Maggiore has been transformed into a palatial island, the work of the Borromeo family.

likeness to a boat was not accidental –
there were plans to give it bows but these
were never built.

From the jetty steps and an octagonal
Gothic folly, the island rises 37 metres
(120 feet) above the water in a series of
terraces, with the retaining walls elegantly
arched. Each terrace is emphasized by
lines of evergreen topiary, and the tiers
of gardens are decorated in the Italian
style with obelisks and marble statues.
A water theatre in the central courtyard
is embellished with statues of the gods,
putti and a prancing unicorn.

Without its lush planting, the island
might look like a marble mausoleum, but,
being surrounded by such a large expanse
of water (Lake Maggiore takes more than
a day to drive around), the island has its
own microclimate. The rainfall is high,

the summers not too dauntingly hot and
tempered by cool breezes, and the winters
mild, despite the proximity of the Alps. The
favourable climate has allowed the plants to
grow quickly, and after three hundred years
the trees are fine specimens and the exotic
planting highly colourful. Evergreens are
clipped into cones and whorls or left to
grow in their natural shapes. There are
brilliant camellias, magnolias, jasmine,
pomegranates and all sorts of citrus trees
and espaliered fruits. Seen from the road,
blocks of brilliant oranges, yellow and
scarlet stand out against the monochrome
background of white marble and dark box
trees. Two notable visitors, Gilbert Burnet
(later Bishop of Salisbury) in 1684 and the
magistrate and scholar Charles de Brosses
in 1739, both agreed that Isola Bella was
one of the loveliest spots on earth.

Opposite, top left Ferns surround a nymph in her
pebble-lined grotto, an essential part of an Italian
formal garden.

Opposite, top right The lake and the nearby Alps are
always visible on the island, providing a contrast with
the formality of the building, statuary and planting.

Opposite, bottom left Like all islands, Isola Bella
is subject to instant changes in the weather, from
romantic mists to full sun.

Opposite, bottom right Statues and obelisks
ornament the buildings on the island, giving its profile
from the shore a series of arches and spikes.

Above The buildings on the island are designed to
take full advantage of the magnificent views of Lake
Maggiore as well as the lushly terraced planting.

Tresco Abbey
Isles of Scilly, England

The Isles of Scilly are the most southerly part of Britain, with a climate that is rarely frosty and a lowest temperature of around 5°C (41°F). However, the islands' gardens do have to cope with violent, salty winds; the Scillies are highly exposed to North Atlantic storms and have been the site of numerous shipwrecks.

Tresco, in the middle of the group of islands, was early populated by monks, who chose it for its freshwater lakes. Attacks by pirates proved too much, however, and in the early fifteenth century they abandoned the abbey they had built. Wild *Narcissus tazetta*, possibly introduced by the monks, flourished among the ruins, and these bulbs later provided the impetus for a trade in early daffodils to the mainland.

The Tresco Abbey garden was begun not by the monks but by Augustus Smith, who leased the island in 1834. Four years later he was living in the house he had designed on a rock high above the rest of the island, and was starting to work on his garden. He began to plant rarities after an appeal by Sir William Hooker, the first director of the Royal Botanic Gardens at Kew. Smith started with mesembryanthemums, and Hooker's son Joseph was 'astonished and delighted with

Tresco has its own microclimate, and palms, azaleas and Tuscan cypresses flourish together.

the luxuriance and variety especially of the Cape and Australian vegetation'. Smith later wrote to friends that he was 'at last finishing up the rocky slope beneath the Abbey at the east end and [had] erected such a vast screen of rough masonry that is fit to be part of Sebastopol, and has been christened the Malakoff, and it is to be crowned by a chevaux de frises [sic] of Aloes'. Actually, these were agaves, not aloes, and they astounded visitors more used to gentle English planting. A postcard from about 1900 shows people dwarfed by these towering, viciously armed succulents, which must indeed have been as effective a barrier as the medieval spiked defence that Smith envisaged.

By 1857 Smith was planning the upper terrace. 'It is to be the chief feature of the gardens and will, I fear, rather make the lower alleys, especially the long walk, not a little jealous.' He planned to raise Neptune on his throne at the top of the grand

staircase, and hoped the eagle – a sculpture of a Mexican eagle in the Mexican garden – would not pick a quarrel. Another area was 'Australia', which 'has some brilliant productions, particularly of the Aralia tribe, Acacias and Cassias'.

The garden, then as now, provided suitable habitats for an enormous range of plants. Proteas and other South African and Australian plants thrived in the shallow soil and full sun at the top of the island, while the moist, shaded valleys were ideal for New Zealand ferns, including *Woodwardia radicans* and *Cyathea medullaris*. Trees and shrubs from all over the world flourish there, from the Canary Island palm, *Phoenix canariensis*, to the scarlet-flowered *Metrosideros excelsa* from New Zealand, helping to make Tresco Abbey one of the most extraordinary gardens in Britain.

The garden is also a time capsule, an example of the work of a Victorian plant collector from a time when wealthy

gardeners could not get enough rare and exotic plants from all over the world. Smith was exceptionally clever in picking Tresco to house his collection, for here he could grow more than anyone else in Britain.

Smith died in 1872 and was succeeded by his nephew Algernon Dorrien Smith, who continued the garden's exotic planting, as did Algernon's son Arthur, a botanist, who took over in 1917. The garden is still owned by their descendants.

Above, left Aeoniums, agaves, nerines and palm trees show how exotic the planting can be in this mild spot.

Above, middle The Smiths collected plants from all over the world to make Tresco a nonpareil Cornish garden. Even proteas can survive in this haven, a testing ground for their hardiness.

Above, right Although the planting is subtropical, the plans and layout remain in the English tradition.

Opposite Palms, a symbol of subtropical gardens, are everywhere on the island because they can cope with strong winds.

Ilnacullin
County Cork, Ireland

Ilnacullin is not an obvious choice for
an island garden. But, against all advice,
John Annan Bryce (1874–1924), a Belfast-
born businessman who had worked in
India and Burma, chose it almost on an
impulse in 1910. Ilnacullin, the Island of
Holly, sits in the delightful Bantry Bay
on Ireland's south-west coast, but it is
battered regularly by storms heaving
in from the Atlantic. Moreover, it had
virtually no soil, so the underlying rock
was barely covered.

Annan Bryce employed the architect
and garden designer Harold Peto
(1854–1933) to design for him a garden
and a five-storey house. This was another
eccentric choice, for Peto was known for
his Italian-style gardens and for lavish use
of belvederes, temples and pavilions, often
filled with genuine antiquities.

From the start, the project was beset
by difficulties. The soil, which had to be
brought from the mainland in boats, could
not be spread deep enough to plant the trees
that were essential to create a shelter belt.
To create planting basins big enough to
accommodate the tree roots, holes had to be
blasted in the virgin rock. This alone took
three years and one hundred men, all of

Ilnacullin in Bantry Bay is also known as Garanish or
the Island of Holly. There was virtually no topsoil here
when John Annan Bryce bought it in 1910.

whom had to be ferried out to the island. Later, it took three boatloads to transport Peto's antiquities, many of which were later sold by Annan Bryce's son Rowland during the Depression.

But the island garden we see today is a triumph. Olda FitzGerald, in her book *Irish Gardens*, says it is often compared to the Garden of Eden, while Patrick Bowe, in *The Gardens of Ireland*, calls it enchanted. This is thanks to Annan Bryce himself, who was called 'a walking encyclopaedia of plants' by the locals. To the first shelter-belt trees of Scots and Austrian pine (*Pinus sylvestris* and *P. nigra*) he later added Californian

Monterey pines (*P. radiata*), which grew 15 metres (50 feet) in ten years. Annan Bryce ignored Peto's planting plans (which tended to be secondary to his structural designs) and set about finding rare plants typical of those at 50 degrees of latitude south of the equator, Ilnacullin being the same latitude north. Bryce was a member of the Royal Geographical Society and knew his stuff.

The garden – 'a botanical Noah's Ark', according to Olda FitzGerald – is filled with plants from New Zealand, Tasmania and Australia, Chile and Argentina, and South Africa. The Chatham Island forget-me-not (*Myosotidium hortensia*) has naturalized,

and a rare Chinese conifer, *Fokienia hodginsii*, also survives. A bottlebrush, *Callistemon salignus* 'Murdo Mackenzie', pays tribute to the head gardener who kept control of the island after Bryce's death in 1924, and there is a tea tree named 'Rowland Bryce', after his son.

At first critics complained that the many buildings on the 16-hectare (39-acre) island were too imposing for the planting (the main house, by the way, was never built), but the soft air and moist climate have now redressed the balance and the rare plants have created 'glorious sweeps of untrammelled Robinsonian plantings', according to Olda FitzGerald.

The garden is now owned by the National Parks and Monuments Service of Ireland and is open to the public, and you have to cross to Ilnacullin by ferry, just as the Bryces and their workmen did.

Opposite, left Bryce's chosen designer was Harold Peto – a strange choice for a barren, rocky, Irish islet, since Peto favoured Classical Italian gardens.

Above Peto designed formal ponds and a gazebo for Bryce, but the house planned for the island was never built.

Right The gazebo is strategically placed so that visitors get sweeping views of Bantry Bay as well as of the formal garden.

THE WATERSIDE GARDEN

Living beside a river or lake has always held an attraction beyond the practicalities of providing water for drinking, washing and the irrigation of crops. Water adds an intangible element to the environment and the atmosphere. The ancient Chinese created vast lakes for their own enjoyment (see pages 27–29), and we know that when Vesuvius erupted in AD 79, there were strings of luxurious villas all around the Bay of Naples, considered to be one of the most beautiful locations in the world. Such villas would have been common near to water throughout the Roman Empire, in Spain, France and even Britain. The Palladian villas on the Brenta Canal near Venice came some 1500 years later but were similar in atmosphere, and they, too, were admired and coveted for their prestigious setting.

Part of the attraction of a waterside setting is the quality of the light. It is not accidental that many artists – for whom the play of light on water, the constant changes in the weather and scenery, are a natural inspiration – have been drawn to settle in waterside locations. The California coast, the Italian Lakes and Collioure, where the Pyrenees meet the Mediterranean, have all proved to be a magnet for artists. In Britain, artists gravitated to the Cornish seaside towns in the nineteenth century, and St Ives and Newlyn have ever since been associated with art. Other artists, including Dame Laura Knight, congregated at Staithes, north of the Yorkshire fishing port of Whitby, and Charles Rennie Mackintosh loved to move between maritime Glasgow and Southwold on the Suffolk coast, which attracted another artistic colony. The French Impressionists would enjoy weekend painting parties on the banks of the Seine, and both James Abbott McNeill Whistler and Claude Monet took regular rooms at the Savoy Hotel in London so that they could capture views of the Thames at sunrise and dusk.

John Ruskin, critic and artist, loved the romantic, dramatic Lakeland hills around his home at Brantwood in England's Lake District.

Some artists also set about creating gardens among the landscapes they painted. John Ruskin, both artist and art critic, installed himself at Brantwood, in England's Lake District, in 1872 and lived there until his death in 1900. The position was superb: the garden ran down to Lake Coniston and the changing light on the slopes of the Old Man of Coniston across the water would vary by the moment. Even Ruskin's bath looked out over the lake. He made a network of paths over his lakeside estate, allowing the walker to come upon sudden dramatic views, and he also created a series of springs, pools and waterfalls fed by a tank in the hills. When guests were expected, the water would be let loose to impressive effect. The garden at Brantwood is filled with vignettes that clearly inspired the meticulous details of nature in Ruskin's paintings and drawings: sprays of ivy on trees, rocks colonized with native ferns, and the small, green, heart-shaped leaves of the moisture-loving wood sorrel (*Oxalis acetosella*). This garden was sadly allowed to decay, but is now well on the way to complete restoration.

Another Victorian waterside garden undergoing restoration is that of the extraordinary Bantry House (below), created by Viscount Berehaven directly on the shores of Ireland's Bantry Bay. Berehaven went on Grand Tours between 1823 and 1843, and considered, rightly, that Bantry Bay was as beautiful as the Bay of Naples and as atmospheric as Lake Geneva. His garden, he decided, should resemble the Boboli Gardens in Florence, but with the added attraction of descending directly to the shore. He imported palms and orange trees, which, in the soft climate of Ireland's west coast, stood a reasonable chance of surviving. Best of all is the huge one-hundred-step staircase, which he had built to romp up the steep hillside behind the house. 'Those who reach the top', says *The Good Gardens Guide*, 'are rewarded with the most stunning view of the house and gardens below and Bantry Bay sweeping out to the broad Atlantic beyond.' Bantry House was a palace in its time, but a series of rakehell owners and some very bad luck meant it fell into near-dereliction. More recently, however, a huge programme of restoration is bringing its garden (which is open to the public) back to life.

As Viscount Berehaven experienced at Bantry, the proximity of a quantity of water moderates the climate, and waterside gardens in the mild south-west of Britain are often subtropical in style. Glendurgan, Carwinion and Meudon on Cornwall's Helford Estuary are full of such exotics as palm trees and the giant umbrellas of the water-loving *Gunnera manicata*, which forms itself into glades. There are theories that the same skilled garden designer planned the winding routes and sudden surprise views that characterize all three gardens, and Trebah (see pages 123–25) is probably another of this set.

The Gulf Stream, flowing up the west coast of Britain from the Caribbean, means that coastal gardens even as far north as Scotland can support exotic plant life. Major J.P.T. Boscawen, son-in-law of the owner of Brodick Castle on the Isle of Arran, arranged for a steamship full of exotics to be brought from his uncle's garden at Tresco Abbey (see pages 107–109). The moisture-laden atmosphere also suits Himalayan exotics: the woodland at Brodick Castle has plants brought over from Achamore (a case of islands helping each other) as well as rhododendrons 'hunted' by the intrepid Frank Kingdon-Ward. Rhododendrons gathered by another great Victorian plant-hunter, Reginald Farrer, flourish at Crarae, on the edge of Loch Fyne (Lady Grace Campbell of Crarae was Farrer's aunt), and the gorge of the Crarae Burn as it tumbles down to the loch could be mistaken for a miniature Himalayan valley (above, right).

While it is always tempting to rise to the challenge of trying to establish plants on the edge of their climatic limits, there is also a trend towards letting things be, and enjoying what nature has to offer. Many waterside gardens hark back to the nineteenth-century Romantic ideal of untouched, or almost untouched, nature. One photographer in Maine is 'gardening' beside a lake in just this way. She loves the wildlife: loons nesting by the shore, squadrons of bufflehead ducks and hooded mergansers, beavers felling trees for their dams. And there is the ice. 'One phenomenon that happens in April', she recounts, 'is that the ice breaks up in the lake and flows with the current to one end. A couple of years ago, the wind changed as this was happening and started pushing the ice to the north, up to my house. … It was extraordinary, little pieces like ice cubes, piling up towards me and tinkling as they rolled over … bizarre and scary.'

So many different factors attract gardeners to the waterside: the gardens in this chapter alone were created variously by a desire for the cool delight of the water itself, the promise of a wonderful habitat for plants and a setting inspired by oriental art.

Opposite Bantry House is perfectly sited so that, from the upper garden, the eighteenth-century house is seen against the background of Bantry Bay.

Above, left The Romans appreciated seaside villas, and a string of them were built for the wealthy around the Bay of Naples. This is the Villa Jovis.

Above, right The damp climate and ragged, rocky coastline of the west coast of Scotland provided ideal conditions for mountain plants being introduced from the Himalayas and China. Crarae on Loch Fyne belonged to relations of the Victorian plant-hunter Reginald Farrer.

Innisfree
New York State, USA

The garden called Innisfree is not what it seems. It is not in Ireland, as one might expect, but in New York State. And it could not be further from Irish scenery, design or plants: it was inspired by Chinese landscape and gardens. This is how it happened.

Originally called Millbrook, Innisfree was the family home of Marion Beck, whose husband, Walter, was an artist and teacher. When they moved there in the 1920s, they changed its name to Innisfree in homage to W.B. Yeats's poem 'The Lake Isle of Innisfree'. Why? The garden has no nine bean-rows and no hive for the honey-bee as the poet suggests, but it held the same promise of simplicity and peace as the poem, which is deeply romantic. What happened to Innisfree is equally so.

The house Marion Beck inherited was surrounded by 300 hectares (740 acres) of rolling hills, natural woodland and outcrops of stone. At its centre was the 16-hectare (40-acre) Lake Tyrrel. Walter Beck, who trained at the Royal Academy of Fine Arts in Munich and later taught at the Pratt Institute in New York, became enthused by black-ink brush paintings of the Chinese landscape and calligraphic scrolls, especially those of Wang Wei, an

Like scholar stones in Japanese and Chinese gardens, these characterful rocks have been thoughtfully placed around the lake at Innisfree.

Left Visitors to gardens should never assume a beautiful corner is down to luck. Like this rocky waterfall with ferns, it will almost certainly have been carefully planned and planted.

Below At the centre of Innisfree's garden is a natural glacial lake.

Opposite, top left Waterspouts do occur naturally, but this one, like much in the garden, is a man-made but appealingly naturalistic addition.

Opposite, top right Rocks, whether used to build outcrops or to provide visual statements, were all collected locally, the debris of Ice Age glacial action.

Opposite, bottom Intimate 'cup' gardens, each separate and distinct, were created to emulate a Japanese 'stroll' garden.

eighth-century artist who used his own gardens and buildings as subjects for his paintings. From 1930 until Marion Beck died in 1959, they used the inspiration of Wang Wei's garden scrolls to create their own garden. Later, their protégé, Lester Collins, a landscape architect whose views coincided with their own, took on Innisfree until his own death in 1993.

Using the natural glacial lake as the garden's centre, the Becks constructed a series of intimate 'cup' gardens, each one separate and distinct from the next and each creating its own self-contained scene. In each, the intention was to create asymmetrical spaces that combined rhythm and pattern with space and form, as in the Chinese scroll paintings they studied.

Because this was to appear a natural landscape, the garden largely relied on plants from the surrounding woods to create the scenery. These were carefully planted and pruned into artistic but natural shapes. The Becks used the rocks left by the glacier – sandstone, limestone, granite and quartz – to make the stone sculptures essential to Chinese gardening. Each was moved into its precisely planned space and positioned to give just the right punctuation mark. Water from the lake was pumped into a huge reservoir hidden in the hillside, from which a series of underground pipes fed the man-made pools, waterfalls and sculptures that enliven each garden 'picture'. Lester Collins's contribution was to apply Japanese skills to these Chinese-inspired pictures. He worked to make links between the various cup gardens, so that visitors would walk from one set scene to another, a concept known as a 'stroll' garden.

Today, the house, which was in the twentieth-century Queen Anne style – somewhat heavy but less lowering than the Victorian country house – has gone. It was demolished in 1982 as not being in keeping with the garden. The garden itself has been reduced to 60 hectares (150 acres), and, since Collins's death, Innisfree has been run by a trust, which opens the garden to the public.

Trebah
Cornwall, England

Three of the best gardens in Cornwall owe their origins to a family of Quakers who moved to Falmouth to start a shipping office. By the early nineteenth century three brothers of the Were Fox family were making a string of lush gardens along the Helford Estuary: Alfred created Glendurgan, now owned by the National Trust; Robert, a fellow of the Royal Society, planted Penjerrick; and Charles (1797–1878) made a life's work of Trebah. These last two are both still in private hands, though Trebah, brought back from dereliction by Major Tony Hibbert and his wife, now belongs to the Trebah Garden Trust.

The garden at Trebah extends over 10 hectares (25 acres), nearly all of it on the banks of a steep ravine leading down to the Helford River. From the Georgian house at the head of the valley and from all points of the garden, the wide river, with its scuds of sailing boats and shipping, can always be seen.

Cornwall's climate is advantageously affected by the Gulf Stream, but Trebah's south-facing valley is additionally protected from the Atlantic's fierce winds. Even before Charles Were Fox began to garden here in 1826 (he first rented Trebah

The Helford Estuary, steep, sheltered and sunny, is the home of some of Cornwall's most idyllic gardens.

from his father, Robert, before finally owning it in 1842), there was a substantial shelter belt around the steep slopes.

Charles Were Fox began by laying out a series of paths, using gravel brought up from the estuary, and these survive, leading tortuously down the steep slopes either side of the ravine. He also began to create a series of pools on the upper, less steep, reaches. From here a rivulet runs virtually the whole length of the ravine garden, a constant in the shifting design.

By the time Charles died, in 1878, the garden was nearly complete, and he left it to his daughter, Juliet, wife of Edmund

Backhouse, another Quaker. In 1904 Edmund Fitzherbert, a garden writer, commented that Trebah could not be excelled for the natural beauty of its surroundings; then, in 1913, *The Garden* magazine described its design: 'sloping banks on either side of the valley are intersected with pathways, but so cleverly has the work been carried out that it is seldom one gets a glimpse of the paths except in the immediate vicinity. … Natural effect is aimed at throughout and successfully secured, harmony of colour and contour being a striking feature.'

Striking, too, is the planting, typical of nineteenth-century woodland gardening, with seas of hydrangeas and large camellias and rhododendrons (two, *R.* 'Trebah Glory' and 'Trebah Gem', are crosses of *R. arboreum* and *R. griffithianum*). The jungle effect is emphasized by a grove of the tallest Chusan palms (*Trachycarpus fortunei*) in the country and an underplanting of tree ferns, some about a hundred years old. Himalayan candelabra primulas revel in the damp soil at the bottom of the ravine, as do the spreading stands of *Gunnera manicata*, which shoots up to 4 metres (13 feet) high in a single season.

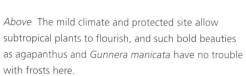

Above The mild climate and protected site allow subtropical plants to flourish, and such bold beauties as agapanthus and *Gunnera manicata* have no trouble with frosts here.

Right, top The gardens on the Helford Estuary incorporate similar paths and streams threading down the steep slopes to the water, persuading experts that a single designer worked on several of them.

Right Water runs down the valley in a series of streams, pausing to broaden into ponds at intervals before reaching the estuary. Tree ferns grow to full height here, bringing the feeling of tropical forest glades to an English garden.

The Hanbury Garden
Ventimiglia, Italy

English gardeners get around, creating extraordinary gardens throughout the world, but while they may make every attempt to fit in with the local traditions, they somehow never quite lose their essential Englishness. So it was with Sir Thomas Hanbury (1832–1907). He was a tea and silk merchant who lived for many years in Shanghai, but as he was travelling through Italy in 1867 he fell in love with a most romantic spot: La Mortola, so named for the wild shrubby myrtle bushes that grew on its slopes. The land, near Ventimiglia on the border with France, was on steeply sloping crags that dropped more than 90 metres (300 feet) to the waters of the Mediterranean, and, sheltered from the north and facing due south, it was perfect for a garden.

Sir Thomas started to buy land on the slopes and develop the site. Much of it had been roughly terraced, and these terraces were improved and stabilized, leaving the old retaining walls in place. Many of the native and fruit-bearing plants – cypresses, olives, lemons and vines – were also kept, as was the ancient Roman Via Julia Augusta, which went through the land.

Sir Thomas Hanbury, a much-travelled merchant, fell in love with the landscape of La Mortola, on the Italian–French border, when he came there in the mid-nineteenth century.

127

When he realized that more could be done with the garden, Sir Thomas called in his brother Daniel, who was a pharmacologist and botanist, and together they experimented with exotic plants, seeing which would flourish in the mild climate. The garden still abounds with exciting mixtures of planting. Within the 45 hectares (112 acres) there are plants from Central and Southern America, South Africa and Australia. There are cycads and succulents of wildly exotic appearance, along with eucalyptus, Mexican cypress, acacias, melaleucas and metrosideros as well as a palm grove, and huge collections of salvias, roses, agaves and aloes, with many more citrus trees than were originally planted. In all, the garden contains six thousand plants, each one of them named.

In addition to the backdrop of the Mediterranean, water is ever-present in the garden itself: streams cascade down the hillside, and a complicated watering system was constructed to irrigate the plants and to feed the pools and fountains that appear among them.

To view his work, Sir Thomas added a tower to the villa within the garden, with stupendous views out over the sea. There are formal belvederes, statues and stairs at various points on the terraces, in the Italian style, but what is English about this garden is its wild abundance within an apparent formality. The cycads and succulents that crowd the upper reaches with bananas and agaves are packed together with Italian cypresses as a dark background; oleanders in violent colours arch over the stream banks; while climbing roses, always at their best in the mild Mediterranean climate, clamber over the terraces. In this, it makes a very obvious contrast with the other, Italian, gardens of the region.

When Sir Thomas died in 1907, the work continued in the hands of his son, Cecil, and wife, Dorothy Symons, and changes were constant. However, when Cecil died in 1937, La Mortola fell gradually into decay and nearly vanished. It was rescued by the University of Genoa, who took it on in 1983 and undertook the huge work of restoration, and the garden formerly known as La Mortola was renamed The Hanbury Garden in recognition of the family's work.

Above, left Sir Thomas and Daniel Hanbury experimented with exotic plants to find out which would thrive in La Mortola's soft climate.

Above The garden's site is perfect – south-facing and sheltered by hills from northern winds – and its many levels provide numerous opportunities for small, self-contained 'pictures'.

Opposite The house is perched on a high point above a precipitous cliff, with the Mediterranean always as a backdrop.

THE TOWN WATER GARDEN

With the obvious exception of the landscape garden, most styles of gardening will adapt to the smaller spaces of town and city. While Versailles may not at first glance appear to be a good example to follow, in fact, taking one element and reducing the scale could work very well. If one looks at George Carter's design for the small London garden of gardens photographer Marianne Majerus (see pages 135–37), one sees all the baroque elements of theatricality and false perspective put to use. In Annabel Astor's London garden (overleaf), on which Carter collaborated with Xa Tollemache, delicate eighteenth-century frostwork creates an eye-catcher at the end of a long, still rill. In my own London garden, a single stone urn acts as a central feature, with water incessantly bubbling over the rim into a very small circular pond. With its surroundings of stone flags, raised beds and clipped yew hedges, it is a formal Italian garden in miniature, its architectural qualities emphasized by such plants as acanthus and figs.

A cottage-garden style would transplant very well into those towns that are built of soft, honey-coloured stone. Re-creating on a modest scale a series of ponds and rills in the style of Gertrude Jekyll and planting with ferns and ivy would be ideal for a sunless basement area. Islamic gardens also provide an excellent template for town gardens throughout the world. Walled and private, they create a restful and practical space, an outdoor room for relaxation. Their classic design of two intersecting rills dividing the space into four beds also fulfils another need of many town gardens: to look good from above.

Both Chinese and Japanese styles of gardening are also ideally suited to towns, largely because so many of the real ones are

This serene space in London, designed by Charlotte Rowe, uses precision-cut stone, wood and lighting to produce a modern take on a traditional formal garden. The planting is lush but restrained, with foliage rather than flowers, and severely trained trees give height and clothe the high walls.

actually town gardens. Tiny fish ponds and bamboo water spouts provide interest and animation in a small space, and taking up the Japanese idea of raked gravel to represent flowing water is restful and does away with the need for a lawn (always difficult to maintain in small town gardens). 'Scholar' stones provide decoration, and areas of uniform pebbles, perhaps arranged around a single tree or a circular pond, are very effective. Peter Walker has combined abstraction with Japanese traditional raked gravel and stepping stones for a garden in the new town of Harima, Japan.

Perhaps the style most suited of all to town gardens is the Minimalist, Modernist school from the Bauhaus onwards. Such architects as Le Corbusier (1887–1965) and Ludwig Mies van der Rohe (1886–1969) made the house and its garden indivisible, with large areas of plate glass without a single glazing bar dividing the two, and with spaces that – half room, half terrace or balcony – further blurred the divide between the garden and house. John Pawson has created a similarly 'barrier-free' house and garden in London, while the plate-glass walls of Baggy House, perched on a cliff in north Devon, are programmed to slide down entirely into the basement on warm days. Other Modernist tricks suited to

town gardens include fabric stretched from one high wall to another for shade on hot days, and, given the right quality of light, painting the walls in strong hues.

In such strong Modernist designs, plants may be felt to be hardly necessary, but if a town garden is to have some aura of peace without plants, it must have water. Water can provide the movement, variation, musicality and serenity that are essential to counter the hubbub of the city – a concept that oriental and Islamic gardeners understood so well.

Given the technology, the town water gardener can indulge in all sorts of high-tech dramas. In Topher Delaney's Che Garden in San Francisco (opposite), a raised pond in the shape of a round table is underlit so that the water pouring over the lip becomes sculptural. In his design for the Plaza Tower in Costa Mesa, California, Peter Walker's concentric circular pools edged in stainless steel are separated by empty roundels into which the water falls smoothly, like a weir, forming a contrast between the mirror effects of the rings of water and the darkness of the empty areas.

Another fine aquatic trick is to use misting machines and lighting together, to create translucent veils of water

wreathing around statuesque plants. The black-stemmed bamboo (*Phyllostachys nigra*) is a favourite for this treatment; indeed, bamboo and water are made for each other. The black, variegated or brilliant-yellow culms are splendid against plain or coloured urban walls, and the elegant leaves, in shadow, irresistibly recall Chinese brush paintings.

The Chelsea Flower Show gardens are an excellent source of inspiration on how to use water on a small scale. In his garden for the *Daily Telegraph* at the show of 1997, Christopher Bradley-Hole made a stairway of water descend from a wall into a rill that ran under a glass bridge. For the show of 2000, designer Stephen Woodhams contrasted the shadows and green translucency of running water by casting a wide veil of water against a white wall.

Water jets that emerge direct from paving have been used to great effect in a number of locations, including the Place des Terreaux in old Lyon, France, and the courtyard of Somerset House, London. The Belgian garden at Annevoie, Belgium, has a more naturalistic variation of this idea; there, small bubbles of water emerge from grassy terraces (see page 63–65). Many designers have taken abstract art as their inspiration, creating Cubist or Rothko-like 'living paintings' with brilliant blocks of

plain colour for walls or planting, and treating water as a form of animate block pages 147–49).

With care, because water in bulk is very heavy, even roof gardens can benefit from a water feature. Here I am thinking of Victor Carrasco's design with a single tree, its trunk painted white, in a square, white-sided container surrounded by water. The tree, which should be carefully chosen, becomes a living sculpture, and the ripples of the pond below light up its leaves and branches with moving shadows.

Water in a town garden always provides the theatricality that is needed to distract from the city beyond, and the opportunities it provides are many and varied.

Opposite, top left George Carter and Xa Tollemache designed this small London garden for Lady Astor.

Opposite, top right Such thuggish plants as bamboo can be controlled in tiny gardens and do well alongside water features and walls. This is a private garden in Gatcombe, Isle of Wight, by Jenny Jones and Timothy O'Brien.

Above Topher Delaney designed this raised fountain-cum-pool with under-lighting, which gives it an entirely different character at night.

133

THE TOWN WATER GARDEN

Clark–Majerus Garden
London, England

The designer George Carter excels himself with town gardens, all of which are dramatic and stylish and invariably make use of water. I have chosen one in Islington, north London, because it is an example of what can be done with very unpromising beginnings.

This pocket handkerchief – it is only 6 × 9 metres (20 × 30 feet) in total – was simply wasteland (a workshop had been built over it) when the gardens photographer Marianne Majerus and her husband, Robert Clark, a lecturer in English literature, bought it in 1986. To some extent, Carter thought this a good thing as there was no need to consider old planting: 'There were no meaningful levels; only the slightly battle-scarred stock London brick walls survived.'

The brief was to make a garden that was simple to maintain, remained interesting throughout the year and made the most of the small space. The design was simple and not outrageously expensive. It is theatrical in both senses of the word: it has drama and it uses stage techniques. The area is raked upwards and has a series of tall, narrow 'wings' constructed of trelliswork; these are back-

This pocket-handkerchief-sized garden in north London incorporates a striking water feature among its other theatrical effects.

planted with such evergreens as holly and yew. The wings grow wider towards the house, creating false perspective to increase the apparent length of the plot. From the house, the areas between the wings are invisible, creating surprises as you walk – no mean feat in a space this size. Shallow lips of brick mark each step of the rake and, because they run horizontally across the space, they make the garden seem larger and squarer than it actually is. The grass is always kept short for the same reason, to give the impression of maximum size.

At the end of the garden is a theatrical eye-stopper. An over-scaled half-urn set against a background of mussel shells is filled with scallop shells. Both sets of shells were arranged and fixed by Majerus and Clark (Islington has good fish restaurants that will happily part with them), using resin glue, and the ensemble – apart from the mussel shells – is painted

a dull grey, imitating lead. From the urn water spills into a small pool, which only becomes visible as you walk up the garden.

George Carter has used a very limited planting plan: evergreens, such as *Trachelospermum jasminoides* (hardy in London), box topiary and camellias for year-round interest, supplemented by restrained additions in each season. The small pond is planted with flag irises (*I. pseudacorus*), and in summer, pelargoniums add touches of white. In summer, too, the garden can be turned into a marquee by simply fixing an awning to each wall and supporting it with a central pole.

Like all successful town gardens, this one looks good from the first-floor drawing-room as well as from ground level. 'It is almost like being seated in the balcony of a theatre,' says Carter. 'From this vantage point there is a better view of the pool into which the urn cascades,

as well as of the gilded glass ball that appears to float on the surface of the water, adding glitter to the garden even on the dullest winter day.'

Above, left The decoration around the lead urn was made by the owners with mussel and scallop shells begged from local restaurants.

Above, right Water lilies and a floating silver ball provide interest in the tiny pool at the base of the urn.

Opposite The ingenious use of evergreen 'wings' hides the narrowness of the garden

THE TOWN WATER GARDEN

The Smith Residence
Sydney, Australia

Town gardens are far more difficult to make effective than country gardens, for space is tight, views, if any, are generally there to be blocked out, the presence of other buildings means light may be a problem, and the soil may be worn out. Town gardens, too, need to be seen from above and, primarily, they need to be dramatic. A small space must pack punch.

The current crop of garden designers who enjoy working in towns have discovered that less is more. Simplicity verging on the minimal, inspiration from the small gardens of the East (especially Japan) and extremely restricted planting are all fashionable options. Add to this an enjoyment of the latest technology and you have the work of one of the current masters of the small space: Vladimir Sitta.

Sitta, born in the Czech city of Brno in 1954, emigrated to Australia in 1984 and, since then, has become one of the most sought-after and influential garden designers in Australia. He insists on using only the finest materials and loves special effects. His gardens may be wreathed in artificial mists, and he uses the reflecting quality of water to bring calm, contemplation and a feeling of space. His work is extremely theatrical and, says

The overhead view is quite different from, but just as satisfying as, the one at ground level.

one enthusiast, he always employs four actors: fire, water, earth and air. Stone is also a feature of Sitta's gardens, especially rough, fissured boulders that contrast with the smooth concrete he also employs.

His most famous garden, the Smith Residence in Sydney, has become a fully lit theatre of surprises. The design is extremely simple: whitewashed walls and the ground covered with water-washed, ochre terracotta squares. Into this space Sitta has placed a long, horizontal waterway. The water gushes from a square travertine marble fountain and cascades over carved steps to reach the long pool in a series of bubbles and foam. From there on the water is still and mirror-like.

This long pool is edged in more smooth marble, a beautiful peachy beige

with a pattern like tree bark, and the same marble, its rough-cut edges uppermost, is made into a series of 'bridges' that span the pool – a regular design feature for Sitta. At one end is a relief sculpture, yet another Sitta signature.

Along one side of the pool there is a simple line of tufty, plain-green mondo grass (*Ophiopogon japonicus*), and along the other, complementing and contrasting with the flopping leaves of the mondo grass, is a line of black-stemmed bamboo (*Phyllostachys nigra*) in a black-covered bed with underlighting for night-time effect. The tall black culms give an asymmetrical pattern to the garden – and to the shadows on the wall behind.

The result is Zen-like in its simplicity and provides a cool oasis of calm within

the city. 'Probably all gardens are romantic,' says Sitta, 'because we believe they will somehow survive us. I would not describe myself as a complete romantic insofar as I believe that my gardens can make a positive impact for change.' He is being proved right in that belief.

Above, left Travertine marble, smooth in the horizontal but rough cut for the bridging slabs, adds creamy colour and bark-like texture to the small space.

Above, right A climber's slender, sinuous trunk makes an architectural statement at the centre of the courtyard, a conscious contrast with the straight lines of the overall design.

Opposite A line of black bamboo, carefully controlled by pruning, provides a year-round screen of greenery, as well as attractive shifting patterns and shadows.

THE TOWN WATER GARDEN

The Dillon Garden
Dublin, Ireland

Helen Dillon's garden in the centre of Dublin had become almost as celebrated for its exuberance and design as had Vita Sackville-West's at Sissinghurst, Kent. For this reason, it is easy to imagine the furore when, at the turn of the millennium, she decided to rip out the famous green lawn that ran down the whole length and replace it with a starkly modern canal of precision-cut limestone. Breath was drawn in, and gardeners' mouths puckered in horror. 'People kept saying "It will tone down in time", but I don't want it to tone down,' Mrs Dillon says. 'I want my garden to make people feel better.' Gardening is not just about good taste, but also about enjoyment.

She and her antique-dealer husband, Val, had become tired of seeing the same 'glumly staring' lawn from the drawing-room window of their Georgian villa, and, inspired by the water gardens of Morocco and El Generalife in Granada (see pages 47–49), they replaced the turf with a smooth sheet of reflecting water. Many gardeners are rebels at heart and Helen Dillon, renowned plantswoman and collector, is clearly one of them.

The strictly formal canal is the main axis, with a series of arches stopping the

In 2000 the garden designer Helen Dillon decided to do away with her lawn and have instead a still canal at the heart of her garden.

vista. The rectangle of water calms the busy, colourful beds and disciplines the garden, taking control of the wildly exuberant planting that sometimes worries Helen as being too overwhelming for visitors ('heavenly muddle' is her expression).

Like the best town gardens (and *The Good Gardens Guide* reckons that this is one of the very best anywhere), this one has a great sense of theatre. 'There's something very dramatic about this garden,' says Helen. 'It's like being in a theatre. We're sitting in a box up here in the drawing-room looking down on the stage below.'

Helen Dillon is a dramatic as well as a romantic gardener. She not only travels to the Himalayas, South Africa, the Alps and New Zealand in search of plants, but also seeks them out in long-forgotten gardens and greenhouses nearer home, and from elderly gardeners. Irish plants, such as *Viola* 'Irish Molly' and *Agapanthus* 'Lady Moore', are favourites, while it cannot be just luck that the garden is next door to the house where the Edwardian plant collector Dr Augustine Henry once lived. The lily that he discovered and which was named after him, *Lilium henryi*, was still flourishing in his garden when Helen and

her husband moved to their present house in the 1970s.

There are huge lessons to be learnt from this town plot: look at the riot of blues in one border – delphiniums, cornflowers (*Centaurea cyanus*), love-in-a-mist (*Nigella damascena*), along with catmints (*Nepeta*) and salvias – contrasting with the magenta and orange across the water, where a richly coloured sea of flowers includes *Knautia macedonica*, *Cirsium rivulare*, *Scabiosa atropurpurea* 'Chile Black' and the wonderful giant *Angelica gigas*. The effect is almost Christopher Lloyd-like in its

radicalism. The comment that 'it will tone down in time' is quite clearly the sort of polite murmur that neither this garden nor this gardener has any time for.

Opposite Helen Dillon's signature dense planting contrasts with the severe stone edging to the canal.

Above Her celebrated Dublin garden is generous for a town plot, at about 0.4 hectares (1 acre) in size.

Above, right Formal bones and sculptures control the exuberant planting, which Mrs Dillon sometimes worries is overwhelming.

Right While many gardeners disapproved of the changes, the new formality has been a triumph.

WATER GARDENS BY TWENTIETH-CENTURY DESIGNERS

During the twentieth century water gardens became essentially architecture-led, much as they had been in the seventeenth century. In earlier times, the patrons of garden architects and designers had been wealthy merchants, aristocrats and royalty, but now patrons appeared in the shape of large businesses or city fathers keen to enhance their profile. Large-scale public projects involved large-scale water features, often conceived to harmonize with the architecture alongside. One thinks, among others, of Walter Burley Griffin's Canberra, with its land and water axes; Valencia's reborn river bed flowing around Santiago Calatrava's curvaceous architecture; and Roberto Burle Marx's landscaped pools reflecting Oscar Niemeyer's Modernist Brasilia.

Although water was a major, sometimes dominant, feature on the public scene in the twentieth century, it played a lesser part in traditional domestic gardens. While plenty of plantsmen and -women were creating gardens, most of them put water features low down on the list of priorities. Even Beth Chatto, who has studied so much about how garden plants behave with and without water in her famous gravel and bog gardens, essentially uses water as a medium for plant cultivation rather than as a decorative accessory. No longer were gardeners using water as an independent character, as sparkling fountains or streams, or as large reflective expanses. Except, that is, in the Modernist mode.

Following the Bauhaus search for 'organic architecture', and such edicts as 'form follows function' and 'less is more', Modernist architects worked in glass, steel and concrete, which suited a new marriage between built and natural environments surprisingly well. Look at Ludwig Mies van der Rohe's Farnsworth House beside the Fox River in Illinois, where the stark exterior of glass and concrete

Brasilia is full of individual Modern architecture, and Roberto Burle Marx has used water in a number of striking, architectural ways both to reinforce and to soften the built environment of this city carved from the rainforest.

merges seamlessly into the surroundings, which, rather than being a garden, are simply green trees and lawns. Frank Lloyd Wright's Fallingwater (see pages 154–57) has an even closer partnership between house and topography. The garden created by the designer Alvar Aalto (1898–1976) at Villa Mairea in his native Finland is essentially a clearing in a forest of dark pines – gardening at the extreme, if you like. The whiteness of the villa is linked to a curvaceous white-edged pool among beds of large daisies. Two willows, *Salix alba* var. *sericea*, create the transition from white garden to dark forest, and sinuous paths wind beside white lacecap hydrangeas and rough grass before the pinewoods take over (above).

If one were to look for influences behind twentieth-century garden design, the finger would point at the Japanese and the Islamic. Aalto's design clearly follows the Japanese way of linking the cultivated garden with its surroundings, and houses by Mies and others were consciously constructed to allow an appreciation of the surroundings in much the same way as were Japanese garden pavilions and monasteries (see, for example, Tenryu-ji, pages 22–25). Further echoes of the oriental can be found in waterside plantings, such as stands of bamboo deliberately placed to cast shadows on blank walls, and the use of stones. These fill beds and raised areas, are used as mosaics in walls and paved areas, and become single decorative objects in the way the Japanese used 'scholar' stones.

The Islamic influence is seen particularly in the treatment of water. In Japanese gardens, water is naturalistic in style: as ponds and lakes, tripping over rocky outcrops or dripping through bamboo pipes. Twentieth-century urban style channels and controls water in a way more akin to the classical gardens of India or Moorish Spain, where it ran in rills bounded by stone or concrete, disciplined and safe (see pages 35–37). Water falls not from rocky walls with splashes and rainbow prisms, but in smooth sheets from squared runnels into square canals, or slides over thick panes of glass, creating optical illusions and shadows as the sunlight catches it.

Controlled nature, a recurrent theme in twentieth-century gardens, draws on aspects of both Islamic and Japanese traditions. Near-Eastern style keeps nature firmly at bay behind walls, and the Japanese Zen philosophy involves minimal planting and precise choice and positioning of each feature. Take, for example, a London garden where a single (though elegant) willow tree is placed, carefully off-centre, in a rectangular bed of water filled with white pebbles. Around it is a floor made of small, square, grey

---

Above, left At Alvar Aalto's Villa Mairea the planting around an irregular pool is kept simple, merging into the dark Finnish forest behind.

Above, right Multiple ledges in Roberto Burle Marx's Fazenda Marambaia in Petropolis, Brazil, create an abstract composition of controlled waterfalls.

Opposite, left This Mexican courtyard by José de Yturbe is a modern take on Mexican traditional architecture, and inspired by such artists as Piet Mondrian and Mark Rothko.

Opposite, right White railings and birch trunks make this cascade by Fletcher Steele at Naumkeag visually memorable.

granite setts, for contrasting texture, and, behind it, green–grey opaque glass cubes are set against white walls. More variation is provided by an open ribbed roof, which, in sunlight, patterns the white walls with diagonals: lovely when the sun shines, less attractive on dull, rainy days. A north London penthouse designed by architectural firm Stanton Williams takes the Minimalist approach one stage further. Huge glass windows lead on to nothing but decking, washed by water to make it glossy and decorated with an arrangement of large, round river pebbles. Not a plant is in sight.

Essentially, these architectural water gardens were treated as rooms, with garden designers thinking in terms of floors, walls and ambience as an interior designer would. Some drew on abstract art for their inspiration, translating a two-dimensional painting into a three-dimensional garden. One in Mexico (above), designed by José de Yturbe, relies on Piet Mondrian-like cubes of colour – ochre, earth red and stone along with shades of black and white – allied to geometric stairs and squares of white pebbles between black paving. A raised pool beside the house is decorated with a bowl of mirrored balls in a niche above the water. The only plants to be seen are beyond the walls. The Cubist garden at Villa Noailles in the South of France, the work of Gabriel Guevrekian (1900–1970), is even more like a Mondrian painting. Seen from above, it consists of a series of squares in black, scarlet and blue, interspersed with squares of green planting in white-edged boxes beside rectangles of reflecting water. Guevrekian was an influence on the American designer Fletcher Steele (1885–1971), whose

garden at Naumkeag, Massachusetts, shows an eye-catching combination of styles (above). For the garden's most famous feature, the Blue Steps, he used white to create form and flow, apparent in the white-trunked birch trees and in the organically shaped white banisters either side of a cascade of blue-painted water spouts. The result is an interesting visual bridge between the blocky colour of Guevrekian and the sinuous, white-highlighted Modernism of Alvar Aalto.

The free forms of Henry Moore's sculpture can be discerned in the gardens of Thomas Church (1902–1978), the father of the California style. At El Novillero in Sonoma County, his kidney-shaped (some say heart-shaped) pool leads the eye to the landscape beyond, where a river meanders through salt flats. A curvy sculpture of white stone sits in the sky-blue pool and a group of heavy, dark trees frames the misty background: the garden as work of art. Although it creates a very different picture, the scene that David Hicks (1929–1998) designed at The Grove in Oxfordshire acts in a similar way: a still rectangle, painted black below the waterline, leads the eye to the countryside beyond.

Ed Bye (1919–2001), on the other hand, brought the American landscape into his Minimalist schemes. He would site rocks within lakes with a truly Zen feeling, incorporating natural woodlands on the water's shores, thus adding a background at the same time as a graphic design that would be mirrored in the still water. One commentator described his work as 'apparently inevitable', as though man had not interfered with nature at all.

GEOFFREY JELLICOE
Shute House
Dorset, England

The garden of Shute House near
Shaftesbury in Dorset is among the most
influential of the twentieth century.
Created by the designer Sir Geoffrey
Jellicoe (1900–1996) when he was in his
late sixties, it combines the experience
and skills of a lifetime of garden and
landscape design with exuberance
and a great sense of fun.

Sir Geoffrey was commissioned by
Michael and Lady Anne Tree in 1968,
shortly after they had acquired the fine
eighteenth-century house. Curiously, it
was Ronald Tree, Michael Tree's father,
who had given Jellicoe his first major
commission – for Ditchley Park in
Oxfordshire – in 1933. Later, Jellicoe was
commissioned by the Duke and Duchess
of York (later King George VI and Queen
Elizabeth) to design the gardens of Royal
Lodge in Windsor Great Park and of
Sandringham, another royal residence, in
Norfolk. Jellicoe also designed the John F.
Kennedy Memorial on the River Thames
at Runnymede, Berkshire, four years
before Shute reached his drawing board.

Unlike his earlier commissions, which
some describe as formal – with strong
axes but unsurprising in concept – Shute

Sir Geoffrey Jellicoe was inspired by visits to Italian
gardens in his youth. This formal scheme marries
Italian and English traditions.

combines all sorts of influences garnered by Jellicoe during his long career. He wrote *Italian Gardens of the Renaissance* in 1925, and there are strong echoes of the Italianate at Shute. More surprisingly, however, the garden also shows a Mughal influence. The centrepiece of Shute must be the musical cascade, a rill that relies on a gentle slope to fall in steps. Between the steps are differently shaped geometric pools, each with a bubbling central fountain. Each waterfall pours into copper bowls that Jellicoe designed to play musical chords. Musical purists rather pooh-pooh this idea, but it makes a pleasant sound. Although a Mughal prince would be surprised to see the lush green lawns that flank the cascade, the running water has the same cooling and calming effect that was intended in Indian gardens.

Water is at the heart of the garden, rising from the natural springs that are used to feed the more formal pools. A larger, still canal is reminiscent of an Italian Renaissance garden, with a series of Classical busts around its edges and massed arum lilies (*Zantedeschia aethiopica*) at one side. Behind the formal walk along the water is a grove of holm oaks (*Quercus ilex*) forming both a dark background and a kind of sacred grove.

The grove, like the garden's natural pond and the viewing platforms he incorporated, shows Jellicoe's romantic strain combining with formality. Elsewhere there are groves of camellias and rhododendrons and, a typical Jellicoe touch, a horticultural 'bedroom' complete with four-poster bed and chequered carpet.

Sir Geoffrey found Shute's marvellous south-sloping site overlooking a pastoral view of Dorset greatly to his taste, and his brief from the Trees was to plan a garden that would 'gently evolve'. He approved of the notion, seeing Shute as 'a laboratory of ideas'. It was his ongoing interest that has created such a beautiful and ingenious garden.

Above The rill, punctuated with square and circular pools, is a clear imitation of the Mughal gardens of India.

Opposite Upstream of the quiet rill, the water is more playful, running from the spring that feeds the garden and plashing down a series of small cascades between luxuriant marginal and bog plants.

FRANK LLOYD WRIGHT
Fallingwater
Pennsylvania, USA

Is Fallingwater at Bear Run (a fine, evocative name) a garden at all? *The Oxford Companion to the Garden* thinks not, denying it any mention, yet Andrew Wilson disagrees and includes its architect, Frank Lloyd Wright (1869–1959), in his book *Influential Gardeners* (2002).

Fallingwater, built deep in the forests of Pennsylvania in 1935 for the rich family of E.J. Kaufmann, a Philadelphia department-store owner, has no garden as we understand the term. What it has instead is an intimate relationship with the wilderness around it. It by no means merges into its surroundings; the architecture of reinforced concrete and horizontal planes is entirely at odds with the vertical lines of the tall trees around it. But, if gardens are intended to delight, enliven, calm and amaze, the architect here has made the wilderness into a true garden. Wright said: 'All the more because I study nature do I revere God, because nature is all the body of God we will ever know.'

Andrew Wilson writes: 'Wright was one of the very few architects of the early twentieth century happy to see their work combined with natural elements.' But

Rather than building to one side of a watercourse, or diverting water to or around a chosen site, Frank Lloyd Wright constructed Fallingwater right over a waterfall.

Wright went further – he bent the elements to his command so that it is impossible to see how Fallingwater was built in that spot at all. Sitting above a mountain stream at the point where it becomes a waterfall, the house is constructed directly on the rock of the forest floor. Indeed, the base of the fireplace in the drawing-room is just this rock, unmoved from its natural bed.

The main features of this iconic building are two huge horizontal terraces, one above the other, at different angles. Of concrete and with walls waist-high, they spring out from the building, a storey higher than the waterfall, which rushes directly beneath them before splashing into a flat pool that gives on to yet another fast-flowing waterfall. The lower of the two terraces forms an extension of the drawing-room, enabling those inside to hear the cascade and see its spray. Above the two main terraces is a third, smaller one, which brings visitors almost under the forest canopy. Those living in Fallingwater, therefore, use the untouched wilderness as their own, private garden.

Fallingwater is not only iconic, but also prophetic. Designed in 1935, it pre-dates Bauhaus architecture, and inspired it, but Wright foresaw that, as the twentieth century moved along, many people would feel the need to return to nature and bury themselves in such remote forests for their pleasure. It is strange but fortuitous that a department-store owner in a provincial city also understood this urge.

Above Fallingwater's garden is the simple forest and lively waterfall. The building's strong horizontals contrast with the spindly tree trunks. Its huge balconies are cantilevered over the water, the sound of which is a constant presence.

Opposite Wright conceived Fallingwater to take full advantage of the seasons of the forest. The site is full of drama, even in winter.

WATER GARDENS BY TWENTIETH-CENTURY DESIGNERS

IAN HAMILTON FINLAY
Little Sparta
Lanarkshire, Scotland

Many of the most influential gardens of the mid-twentieth century were designed by artists rather than gardeners, and this is the case with Little Sparta, created in the beautiful if unfriendly landscape of the Pentland Hills, south of Edinburgh. It was the work of Ian Hamilton Finlay (1925–2006) and his wife, Sue. Finlay was an extraordinary polymath. He was born in Nassau, where his father was apparently a rich bootlegger, but he returned to Scotland as a child, studying later at Glasgow School of Art. He was a sergeant in the Royal Army Service Corps, a shepherd and a farm labourer, which may explain his affection for the landscape, and later (in the 1950s and 1960s) a poet, publisher and short-story writer.

But his life's work was Little Sparta, to which he and his wife moved in 1966. It was then called Stonypath, a name descriptive of its atmosphere. The name change in 1978 was caused by a long-running and aggressive dispute with the local authority, Strathclyde. The council refused to recognize the garden as a work of art and confiscated several sculptures in lieu of business rates (he had accepted a few paying visitors). The state of war

The lonely landscape of lowland Scotland is allowed full rein at Little Sparta. The carvings increase the sense of desolation.

between the parties led to Little Sparta being decked with hand-grenade finials on its gates and a nuclear submarine peeping out from the bushes. So the garden is not only a celebration of the Scottish landscape with its bleak windswept moors, rush-choked bogs and natural lakes, but also a political statement, a successor to eighteenth-century gardens, such as Stowe, that sent a message to those who visited them.

Politically, Little Sparta is intended to make visual Finlay's criticism of modern values and his approval of those of the Age of Enlightenment. Louis de St Just, a leading thinker during the French Revolution, was Finlay's hero, and a series of tablets beside a lake, the climax of the garden, quotes him: 'The Present Order is the Disorder of the Future' (above). St Just championed Roman

virtues and Finlay, too, revered the pastoral values of Virgil.

Finlay filled Little Sparta with beautifully carved stone tablets with meaningful and often witty inscriptions. For example, alongside a grove of silver birches is a tablet inscribed 'Bring Back the Birch' (opposite), while a marshy area has a tablet bearing the words 'See Poussin Hear Lorrain', a reference to his admiration for those Classical landscape painters.

The garden, however, is not all marsh and admonitory stone tablets, for the planting is intended to soften the messages and, sometimes, to throw them off-balance. It is almost cottagey, full of flowers, mown paths and shady, tree-lined areas that create a sense of security – a sense abruptly shattered by the visual messages.

Ian Hamilton Finlay created at Little Sparta a garden that celebrates the

untouched landscape and the values of truth and justice, and reflects his own philosophy. It makes other twentieth-century gardens seem tame.

Above, left A sculpted quotation from St Just, a hero of the polymath Ian Hamilton Finlay, is given a backdrop of Scotland's Pentland Hills.

Above Little Sparta is a complex combination of the formal and informal.

Opposite, top right Informal stepping stones meander across a stretch of water. One reads: 'Ripple n. A fold. A fluting of the liquid element'.

Opposite, bottom left Finlay had a sense of humour: in Scotland the birch rod was long used for corporal punishment in schools.

Opposite, bottom right The modest cottage at Little Sparta sports mock columns and more inscriptions: 'His Music, His Missiles, His Muses' between the columns and, on the window gable, 'Io Apollo'.

WATER GARDENS BY TWENTY-FIRST-CENTURY DESIGNERS

There are clear signs that the twenty-first century is already evolving a new garden style of its own. Certainly, Brutalist elements – concrete, walls of caissons, plantless gardens – are still being created, but I think there is a new sense of fun around.

By fun I do not mean the kind that produces huge statues of unlikely naked women made out of broken old cups, regrettably part of current design, or the updates of the seventeenth-century 'water jokes' that technology has made ever more possible. I do not see that modern life considers such japes to be funny; we like to be spectators rather than victims. But I do enjoy that same technology when it allows designers to be playful with water effects: a still pool that erupts into volcanic action at the touch of a switch; falling water changing from a soundless sheet to a raging torrent. One garden, by Julie Toll, has piles of mossy boulders at the water's edge with steam drifting among them: mystical and evocative (left; designed by Thomas Nordstrom and Annika Oskarsson). Another, seen at the Chaumont garden festival in France (a major source of inspiration among designers), had slabs of stone, their edges still bearing the marks of the quarry, with mist forming and reforming from the gravelled base, catching the sun in rainbow patterns.

Advances in lighting technology have also produced some inventive, playful effects. Lighting can take advantage of both the smooth sheen of the silent flow of water and the dramatic glitter of airborne droplets. Lit from below, fountains and overflowing pools are utterly changed in form.

Modern garden designers, many of whom are trained as architects, are very aware of the effect of natural light and colour. Inspired by the work of the twentieth-century Mexican designers, they might paint walls around pools in strong, complementary

Modern technology has enabled designers to create effects that were once the preserve of nature. In this garden by Julie Toll, steam drifts across mossy boulders: mist on demand.

colours: pink and sky blue, earth shades of ochre and terracotta, or – in hot, dry areas – clashing shades of crimson, orange and purple. These, lit during the day by the sun and the light reflecting from the water, will change dramatically at night, with artificial lighting designed to cast shadows and emphasize plants and architectural features. I love, too, Hockneyesque pools in which the bases are patterned to exaggerate the shadows of ripples.

The combination of water and stone continues to be an important design feature. In a tiny walled city garden surrounded by high whitewashed walls, huge plates of the darkest grey slate are arranged as vast stepping stones with rectangles of still water in between. A few water plants are the only decoration. In a Mexican garden a stone sculpture by Curro Ulzurrun, a broken rectangle with a line of small holes, is used as a spout for a gush of water issuing from a sky-blue wall into a wonderfully inviting pool. This and other long, rectangular pools in the garden are based on agricultural water troughs, and the surrounding planting is suitably tropical.

Californian garden designer Topher Delaney uses plants, but with fierce control. I admire her Californian courtyard in which nine blocks of raised beds are planted with almost nothing but white arum lilies (*Zantedeschia aethiopica*), each of which sits in a white concrete surround filled with white pebbles. These in turn sit in a chequered pattern in a square pool. The only other plants are an elegant bamboo and a flowerless green climber (opposite). In Spain, Victor Carrasco employs a similar style, planting a lemon tree, its trunk painted white, in a white cube of concrete. The concrete bed is surrounded by a sheet of ice-blue water backed by pure-white walls. This pays homage to Spain's Moorish gardens, with their cool reflective pools and enclosing high walls.

These works are clearly sculptural, and this description extends to other modern water features, where the shape of the water is combined with other elements to create more than just a pool. Tadao Ando, for instance, sinks a circular pool into the ground and has water bubbling up in its centre so that one imagines it is a borehole or spring. The sculptural quality is clear throughout the garden when one sees it from above, too: a series of concentric rings of grass and water, a plain pond with a cone-like fountain and a clear, still rectangle of water set at an angle to it.

Another major influence on today's designers is the infinity pool, which may or may not be used for swimming (well-designed swimming pools are now accepted as integral to a garden's design, not a jarring but functional add-on). One of the most beautiful is designed by Oehme, van Sweden & Associates for a garden in Maryland. The garden overlooks a serene bay and the pool replicates the cool, grey water in its stillness and shape, with decking around the edge complementing the vernacular clapboard outbuilding that stands nearby. There is nothing else but a lawn and a pair of ancient oak trees, which happily frame the essential view. In Switzerland, Anthony Paul has used decking for perspective, lining up not with an infinity swimming pool but with the whole of Lake Lucerne (above, left). Spiky palms at once complement and contrast with the jagged outline of the icy Alps, seen beyond.

Above, left Infinity pools are another example of modern technology opening up design possibilities. This well-placed pool by Anthony Paul in Lucerne draws the eye to the mountain range beyond.

Above There is a huge playfulness in current garden design, especially in water features. These jets are in a private garden in Auckland, New Zealand, by Ted Smyth.

Opposite Californian designer Topher Delaney was inspired by Zen Buddhism for this town garden: white arums in square white tubs within a white square of water.

WATER GARDENS BY TWENTY-FIRST-CENTURY DESIGNERS

SIMON IRVINE
**Vinsarp
Västergötland, Sweden**

In eighteenth-century Sweden, outside the main cities, water was the preferred means of transport, and there has always been plenty of it to navigate. So the first view guests would have had as they arrived at the isolated manor house of Vinsarp, in the lake-strewn wilderness north-east of Gothenburg, would have been from the shores of Lake Vinsarpssjon. This was a view designed to impress: the garden in front of the elegant Palladian-style wooden house and the defensive stone tower was laid out in formal, eighteenth-century style.

Vinsarp manor, still formal and made of wood, though much altered over the years, has recently become a holiday home for its owners, their friends and paying guests, and the garden has been designed for them by Simon Irvine, a Briton who has lived long enough in Sweden to understand its fearsome climate and enthralling summers. The first frosts can come, he says, in early September, and by midwinter it might be -15°C (5°F). Even ivy is unable to grow in the wild. By contrast, during the long, light days of the short growing season (between May and September) the plants' growth is phenomenal.

Sweden is a country of lakes, and guests would generally arrive at this remote eighteenth-century manor house by boat.

To him, this wild northern landscape, with its elms, ashes, oaks and wild juniper dotted in rocky green meadows, has extraordinary beauty. The wildlife is stupendous: storks, eagle owls, deer and moose are common sights, along with stubby little Icelandic ponies, which do a lot of agricultural work. The driveway to the house (road rather than lake is today's normal way of arriving) travels through this wild terrain, which, along with a closeness to and enjoyment of nature, is incorporated into Irvine's designs. A romantic, he uses ancient drystone walls and typically Swedish open horizontal fences at the edges of the estate, gradually bringing in formality nearer the house.

The planting is almost entirely annual, as virtually nothing can survive the winter. At Vinsarp, Irvine has followed the traditional Swedish love of light in both quantity and quality. Most of the planting is of the softest green with white flowers: the hazy leaves of cosmos and the luminous flowers of nicotiana are laid out in symmetrical beds with sentinel box topiary and lollipop standards at focal points. These impose a light-hearted screen between the rooms of the house and the views to the lake beyond. Gravel paths lead towards the water, and there are mature trees in the park. Irvine has planted an avenue of limes (*Tilia*), which is already adding to the formality of the main garden even though the trees' trunks

have to be protected against the winter frosts with overcoats of straw.

The vegetable garden, still within its eighteenth-century walls, stands apart from the house, in view of the lake. It is a riot of colour from nasturtiums (*Tropaeolum majus*), marigolds (*Calendula*) and mallows (*Malva*) with grey-leaved artichokes, and catmint (*Nepeta*) for formal edging, contrasting with the huge yellow flowers of creeping courgettes. A charming range of greenhouses contains pelargoniums.

Vinsarp is, of course, a summer house. Its garden vanishes in winter and the lake, so welcoming in summer, freezes over. Visitors would not think of venturing here when the hard frosts come.

Opposite The large lake and feeder streams shape the landscape around the house, which has always been used only in summer.

Top Drystone walls made with huge boulders are a traditional local style of boundary walling; here they help emphasize the delicacy of the wrought-iron gate.

Above Sweden's summer is short and intense. The small formal garden at Vinsarp, designed by Simon Irvine, relies on annuals for its colour.

Above, right Lavender can survive the climate, and makes a blooming hedge in the vegetable garden.

Right Vinsarp's garden is formal, as are the garden buildings. The pretty pavilion at the centre of a range of greenhouses is very much in the Swedish tradition.

CHARLES JENCKS
Garden of Cosmic Speculation
Dumfries & Galloway, Scotland

No one knows why our prehistoric
ancestors built the huge earthwork of
Silbury Hill, Wiltshire, and I suppose it
is frivolous to suggest that it might have
been a Neolithic garden designer. But
these and other earthworks found all
around Britain certainly have an eerie
beauty that is also found at the Garden
of Cosmic Speculation. It has been
proposed that Stonehenge and other
stone circles were constructed to relate to
the movements of the sun and stars and
to celebrate the solstices, and the work
of Charles Jencks and the late Maggie
Keswick at Portrack House has the same
scientific underpinning and the same
ordered but mysterious beauty.

Jencks and Keswick were enthusiasts
of *feng shui* and its use in Chinese
gardens, and also of the Taoist idea
of sculpting land to release the earth's
invisible forces. In the 1990s Jencks began
experiments in 'cosmological' gardening.
The progress of the expanding universe,
he explains, is now thought to be in
sudden unpredictable jumps rather than
a fundamental orderliness. 'Nature is
basically curved, warped, undulating,
jagged, zigzagged and sometimes crinkly.'

Scientific theories of the universe are the basis of
the shapes and dispositions of this fascinating and
individual garden.

The garden, says fellow designer Kim Wilkie, has two motifs: the wave that warps and folds in on itself, and the twist, a symbol for coherent energy.

Cosmology and astrophysics may seem tough concepts both to understand and to portray in a garden, but that at Portrack is evocative and beautiful enough for the most ignorant non-scientists among us. The best-known part of the garden is the series of turf terraces, ziggurats with spiral turf paths that control and balance the curving pools and grass walks between them. These are inspired by fractal geometry. Elsewhere, the double helix of DNA is recalled in a cascade and in metal sculptures. A red bridge over a moorland stream, with the hills of the Scottish Borders in the background, is a reference to the theory of dynamic flux (although, to the untrained observer, the bridge's red metalwork and lattice spars are clearly inspired by early Chinese gardens – a neat combination of the two influences brought to bear at Portrack by Jencks and Keswick). Another well-known part of the garden is made with a mixture of AstroTurf and curving diamonds of metal and symbolizes energy emerging from a black hole.

Kim Wilkie believes that Portrack House carries echoes of the work of Charles Bridgeman both at Claremont (see pages 79–81) and at Stowe, where earth was moved to create complex terraced amphitheatres. This garden is certainly complex in its meaning and in its structure. As Jencks himself says, 'Gardens shouldn't be easy to understand, allowing one to race through them. The point is to appreciate them slowly.' However, as others have found, you no more need to be an atomic scientist to appreciate the Garden of Cosmic Speculation than you need to be deeply informed about Classical myth to enjoy Stourhead (see pages 75–77).

Above Curved ziggurats and precisely shaped terraces and pools are inspired by fractal geometry.

Opposite, top While you do not need to be a cosmologist to appreciate the beauty of the garden, Charles Jencks would like visitors to be thoughtful about its meanings.

Opposite, bottom The work of Charles Jencks and Maggie Keswick harks back to gardens with a message, such as Stowe and Claremont, although this colourful pavilion owes more to the designs of Gerrit Rietveld.

FERNANDO CARUNCHO
Mas de les Voltes
Cataluña, Spain

It is surprising how few of today's great garden designers actually set out to be such; they often began as artists, architects, writers, hobbyists and thinkers. One of the most influential today is Fernando Caruncho, who trained as a philosopher. With a deep interest in pre-Socratic Greece and our relationship with the natural world, he grew to believe that gardens acted as a way into an ancient world, in which we were more intuitive and at one with nature. Gardens were spiritual and consoling.

As a result, Caruncho went to the University of Madrid to train in landscape design, and, in 1979, created a small private garden for a house at the edge of the city. From then on, he is considered to have renewed, single-handedly, the interest in gardening and private gardens among Spaniards. Although most of his work is for private clients, he has also designed gardens for the University of Deusto in Bilbao and the Spanish Embassy in Tokyo.

This last was an inspired choice for, although Caruncho's gardens are not overtly Japanese in mode, his thoughtful, philosophical approach is very much to the Japanese taste. So, too, is his avoidance of colour. This is evident in one of his most

Fernando Caruncho trained as a philosopher, and his gardens, although of the twenty-first century, have an eighteenth-century thoughtfulness about them.

175

famous gardens, Mas de les Voltes, which brings together the traditions of the Mediterranean, the Moorish influence that is so strong in Spain, and Classical design from both Greece and Italy. However, as Andrew Wilson says in his book *Influential Gardeners* (2002), 'his gardens have a serene formality that relates to the historical influence of Islam yet they are distinctly of the twentieth century: clean, uncluttered, expansive spaces full of light and reflective surfaces. Caruncho is not given to nostalgia.'

At the centre of this exciting garden are four square, still ponds, forming a larger square quartered by paths. These clearly hark back to the *chahar bagh*. The garden then develops from this with a single leaping idea: a pattern of flat wheatfields that are at once part of the garden and part of the landscape around it. The fields are carved into geometric designs, each bordered by a lush, green, grassy path. And, of course, the wheat changes with the seasons, from brilliant green in spring to waving golden stalks in autumn; these are then harvested, leaving the landscape bare over winter.

This is deliberate, for it chimes with the countryside and the rhythm of the farming year. Olives line the paths, as they would in the countryside, and dark regiments of tall, pencil-thin cypresses make architectural statements, as they have for centuries. Mas de les Voltes epitomizes everything that inspires and motivates Caruncho: it is cerebral, it is ancient in its inspiration, it uses traditional Mediterranean food plants – olives, vines, wheat – and it breathes the spareness of Modernism.

Above A quartet of square lakes in the *chahar bagh* style form the still centre of a Mediterranean landscape.

Opposite, bottom Olive trees are an enduring symbol of civilization and appear throughout the garden at Mas de les Voltes.

Left A most original aspect of the garden is the series of square, grass-framed wheatfields that surround it, turning from green to gold as the seasons progress.

177

OEHME, VAN SWEDEN
& ASSOCIATES
Still Pond
Virginia, USA

James van Sweden and Wolfgang Oehme, one of America's grandest garden-design teams, have been working together since 1977, and in that time have created dozens of gardens where water is the central theme. Indeed, in 1995 van Sweden wrote a book entirely devoted to the subject. His inspirations, he said, included such diverse artistic expressions as Monet's garden at Giverny (see pages 91–93) and the swimming-pool pictures of the Bradford-born, California-resident David Hockney (who, I imagine, has inspired many gardeners). England, too, has been an inspiration, including the gardens at Stowe and Chatsworth, and the 'grand scale' of the promenades along both sides of the Thames. Another major influence was Frank Lloyd Wright's Fallingwater (see pages 154–57). 'Wright succeeded in closely tying the house to its rugged setting. Fallingwater inspired me to look at setting as well as structure,' van Sweden explains.

Nowhere is this more apparent than at this garden on a horse farm in the beautiful country of Virginia's Blue Ridge Mountains. The garden not only uses water as its theme but also merges its planting and contours with the pastures

Oehme, van Sweden & Associates has taken the stupendous backdrop of Virginia's Blue Ridge Mountains into the design.

179

and hills beyond. Furthermore, and, perhaps uniquely among water gardens, this one has been designed so that wheelchair users can circumnavigate the whole and even reach the water of the pool.

Still Pond, the name given to it by the owners after the garden was finished, has three separate water features. The rustic farm pond, in a calm meadow and with its own gazebo, greets visitors as they arrive at the farm. Boardwalks, sometimes on stilts but always kept nearly level for wheelchairs, circle this, then continue to a terrace with its own lily pool and, finally, to a nautilus-shaped swimming pool that looks wonderfully natural in the landscape.

The swimming pool has a sensational view over the distant mountains, and the surrounding planting is carefully chosen to merge with this backdrop. *Sedum* 'Herbstfreude' is planted alongside

Miscanthus sinensis 'Malepartus' and *Pennisetum alopecuroides*, both tall, natural-looking grasses. The garden, writes van Sweden in his book, is intended 'to complement, not compete' with the scenery – and it does. 'I used the swimming pool and its terrace in their own world on the "view" side of the house, about 18 inches [45 centimetres] lower than the main terrace. By stepping down to the pool and terrace, carefully laying out the hahas and planting up the pool on one side, we managed to pull the pasture right up to the house. From the terrace, it appears as if the horses could come drink directly from the pool.'

The farm pond, which was already there when Oehme and van Sweden came to design the garden, was given a concealed dam, and the planting gradually spreads into the adjoining pasture. 'The boardwalk,

which encircles the edge of the pond, meanders among the plantings and sometimes disappears completely. Finally, the pond reflects the native and newly introduced trees that surround and anchor it firmly into its site. The sounds of bullfrogs and geese from the small offshore island complete the scene.'

Not quite: when the pond's water level sinks in the summer, the revealed edges provide a 'race track' for running the dog.

Above Still Pond has three separate pools. This formalized version of a rustic pond in a meadow is the first that visitors see.

Opposite, top The planting of the garden has been carefully planned to complement the rural scenery beyond. Here, rudbeckias are planted beside grasses.

Opposite, bottom Strong yellow and rusty orange daisies provide blocks of hot colour to emphasize the cool blues of the mountains beyond.

THE WATER GARDEN OF THE FUTURE

The story of water gardening may be about to turn full circle. If the dire predictions of climate change, global warming and melting ice-caps are to be believed (and it seems they are), then we will have to approach water gardening in a new and enlightened way. But this is exactly what the Babylonians, Sumerians and Persians were practising centuries ago. Water was precious to them, too, but that did not preclude their use of it in gardening. Indeed, in arid regions water is all the more valuable in horticulture, so it is used with flair and care.

There are plenty of lessons to be learned from the past. The fountains and garden pools of towns and private estates from the deserts of Anatolia to the arid interior of Spain were supplied from underground water cisterns, which also supplied the residents' basic needs. (Numbers of these tanks still survive, including the enormous cisterns that kept the whole of Istanbul watered.) Gardeners are beginning to think in these terms again, expanding their ideas from water butts to underground reservoirs that will conserve rainwater from the storms we are told will be increasingly likely. The Romans' comprehensive network of conduits and aqueducts sets an example to modern hydraulic engineers of what can be done to transport water from areas of plenty to drier regions.

Gardens are likely to get smaller. While vast hunting parks and rolling landscaped grounds developed in temperate or rainy regions, the gardens in arid areas of the world tended to be walled, jewel-like in their complexity, and focused on rills and canals. I see the *chahar bagh*, the Persian paradise garden, being a valuable template in the future. A modern example with all the attributes of the *chahar bagh* has been created by Martha Schwartz at the Dickenson Residence, in the arid surroundings of Santa Fe, New Mexico. Two intersecting rills, one edged with blue mosaic tiles, the

Arizona has always prized water, and we all may need to in future. Steve Martino's Stiteler Garden shows how to celebrate it.

other with coral tiles, channel water over more blue tiles to enhance the colour of the water. At the centre is a raised brick platform with a green-lined single-jet fountain. The 'beds' are of a fine, light gravel and the only plants, two sculptural trees, have their roots covered with white-painted boulders, to conserve moisture.

I foresee that the owners of large gardens will designate a small area to be the 'real garden', the *chahar bagh* or *hortus conclusus*, which will be walled around and treated as a real oasis for relaxation and contemplation. Outside this will be whatever the land can easily sustain, whether it is orchards or woodland, meadows or arable land.

Above, left While Japanese gardens have changed little over the centuries, the age-old style is being adopted internationally as its admirable use of limited space becomes appreciated. This Chelsea show garden of 2000 is by spidergarden.com.

Above, right Enormous technological changes are fully exploited by new designers, and lighting is one area where this is evident.

Left Simple plants, such as moss, are serene and cooling, and represent a future trend. We will yearn after natural beauty.

Opposite Gardens are becoming a mixture of styles, mingling exotic planting with formal tubs and pools, such as this small swimming-pool plot in the USA.

Perhaps our water gardens will become like today's town gardens. In a London garden that may only be 25 metres long and 4 or 5 metres wide (80 × 15 feet), for example, it is quite possible to create a formal Italian garden with a fountain and a canal between clipped hedges, or a layout quartered with rills and heavily planted with herbaceous plants the colours of a Persian carpet, or yet again an oriental garden with stone temples, raked gravel and tiny dripping stone spouts.

Modernist and Minimalist gardens, of course, come into their own in this situation. Akin to Zen oriental gardens, the Minimalist plot requires very little energy or maintenance, but it does involve modern technology. Such designs use sheets of glass or synthetics, and water can run down these surfaces, glinting in the sun during the day and, at night, lit from behind in a choice of colours. Water can spurt and fountain at the push of a button, peacock-tail fans can enliven still ponds, and bubbling water can appear as if by magic, all created by electronics rather than gravity. Where water is the main feature, planting can be minimal. A globally warmed future has no place for water-hungry lawns or annual plants, but entertainment and colour can be created by using water in its many moods.

We will probably want more swimming pools, but I hope the trend will be to make them look like still pools rather than vulgar turquoise show-offs. Lining pools in dark greys and neutral blues so that they retire into the background rather than shout their presence seems a positive move in design terms, and natural swimming pools are already beginning to gain ground. These not only blend into a garden, but also rely on plants and a balanced eco-system, rather than chemicals, to keep the water clear and healthy.

In some ways this is not a particularly encouraging view of the future, but it is one where the paradise of the garden is more recognized than it is today, and where its benefits are better understood. Whatever the drama of the future, whatever the scientists prophesy, the importance of water in the garden cannot be overestimated. In a world of increasing tension, when many things are uncertain, there is a growing need to be able to retire to a private plot where serenity reigns, where the day's frustrations can be soothed by the quiet trickle of water into still pools and the delight of spraying fountains as the drops of water catch the sunlight. This may, for the privileged few, be a professionally designed personal oasis, or it may be a simple off-the-peg water feature. But, as even the creators of tiny *pen jing* gardens in China knew, water in the garden adds an element of magic.

PLANTS FOR WATER GARDENS

Acer palmatum 'Shindeshojo': typically Japanese in habit and leaf form.

Angelica gigas: wonderfully decorative and loves moist soil.

Nymphaea 'Golden West': the perfect water lily for still ponds.

Rodgersia podophylla 'Longacre': a decorative water-lover with elegant large leaves.

Sedum spectabile 'Herbstfreude': late-summer flowers are worth the wait.

Zantedeschia aethiopica: the arum lily is surprisingly hardy and good near water.

In Islamic, formal and landscape gardens, the water is left unplanted. Landscape-style lakes and rivers are often colonized by reeds and rushes, but this is not the intention.

ORIENTAL GARDENS

The Chinese typically use plants en masse, with one variety providing a block of colour. They also love plants in decorated terracotta pots standing on high bases. The following plants are all used in Chinese water gardens, some around the edges and some in the water itself.

Acorus calamus (sweet flag)
water lilies (*Nymphaea* spp.); see also below
Iris japonica
Weeping willow: varieties of *Salix babylonica*
Bamboos, including *Chimonobambusa quadrangularis*; *Phyllostachys nigra*, *P. aurea* and *P. edulis*; *Bambusa multiplex*
Climbers such as *Ficus pumila*, a twining relation of the fig; *Parthenocissus tricuspidata* (Virginia creeper, called Mountain Climbing Tiger in China); and *Wisteria sinensis*, especially 'Alba'
Fruit trees, especially those in the *Prunus* genus. Typical examples are: *P. salicina*, a plum; *P. triloba*, an almond; and *P. pseudocerasus*, a cherry.
Trees and shrubs might include *Acer palmatum*, *Aesculus chinensis* (Chinese chestnut), *Cotinus coggygria*, *Fatsia japonica*, *Liquidambar formosana*, *Mahonia fortunei* (which the Chinese call Ten Great Virtues), *Musa basjoo* (the hardiest of the bananas), *Osmanthus fragrans* (a beautiful, fragrant shrub, with which the Chinese flavour a tea), and *Trachycarpus fortunei* (Chusan palm).

ROMANTIC GARDENS

There are some excellent trees and shrubs for Romantic gardens on the large scale.

Willows

Willows of all kinds are ideal. Site weeping types so that the tree is reflected in the still water below and wind catches the trailing branches. In addition to *Salix babylonica*, another good weeper is *Salix* × *sepulcralis* var. *chrysocoma*. Crack willow, *S. fragilis*, with its fragile joints, is a traditional holder of watercourse banks, and *S. alba* var. *sericea*, silver willow, is graceful and beautifully coloured.
For coloured winter stems, try *S. alba* 'Cardinalis' or *S. alba* var. *vitellina* 'Britzensis', which have brilliant coral twigs; *S. daphnoides* and *S. acutifolia* for striking dark stems; and *S. gracilistyla*, which has branches of olive green. Another curiosity – though it is just that – is *S. babylonica* var. *pekinensis* 'Tortuosa', the twisted willow, which makes good cut twigs indoors.

Other trees and shrubs

Further up the banks, especially in hilly gardens, silver birches (*Betula pendula*) look fine planted with dark yews (*Taxus baccata*) and holly (*Ilex* spp.), perhaps along with *Populus trichocarpa*, the Balsam poplar, for its wafts of delicious scent. *Populus* × *canadensis* 'Aurea' has golden stems and (says the queen of the damp garden, Beth Chatto) is excellent planted alongside the white willow (*Salix alba*). She also recommends the cut-leafed alder, *Alnus incana* 'Laciniata'.

Foliage interest

The romantic garden would, of course, have ferns and ivy beside tiny waterfalls and creeping out of stone banks. The hart's-tongue fern (*Asplenium scolopendrium*) seems capable of growing virtually in water and in cracks in the stone. I love the wiry growth of the maidenhair fern (*Adiantum venustum*), which never gets big but is exceptionally dainty and very Ruskinesque. The lady ferns (varieties of *Athyrium filix-femina*) are elegant and fresh-coloured.

With ivies, I would stick to non-variegated varieties, which look more natural. I love *Hedera helix minima*, with tiny leaves, the deeply veined *H. donerailensis* and any with giant saucer-sized leaves.

When it comes to herbaceous foliage there are some stunners. Beside a large lake *Gunnera manicata* makes an incomparably bold statement. It can reach the height of a small tree in mild regions and, if covered, will cope with frosts in all but the very coldest regions. *Rheum palmatum*, a relation of the edible rhubarb, is not quite so huge but still very striking, as is the airier angelica (*Angelica gigas*), which you can find with reddish-purple stems and flower buds. Rodgersias love damp soil and their large, five-fingered leaves contrast well with their feathery plume flowers.

Eryngium maritimum: ideal for salty and sandy areas by the sea.

Thrift: a British native that loves the seashore. Neat and colourful.

Olea europaea: the grey-leaved olive is native to – and evocative of – the Mediterranean.

Phyllostachys nigra: the black-stemmed bamboo, essential to modern, Minimalist plans.

Salix alba var. *vitellina* 'Britzensis': blazing-red stems beside the water cheer up winter.

Gunnera manicata: biggest herbaceous plant. Almost hardy beside water in Europe and North America.

ISLAND GARDENS

Gardens beside the sea need special plants to cope with the wind and the salt. *Olearia scilloniensis* comes from the Isles of Scilly and is a neat plant with daisy-like flowers. Most sedums are good, and *S. spectabile* one of the best (and spectacular, as its name suggests). Grey plants, such as senecios, lavenders and artemisias, cope well, as do *Helichrysum italicum* (curry plant), *Stachys byzantina* (lambs' ears) and many brooms (*Cytisus* and *Genista*). So, obviously, do plants that grow by the sea in the wild, such as thrift or sea pink (*Armeria maritima*), sea kale (*Crambe maritima* and its larger cousin, *C. cordifolia*) and sea holly (*Eryngium maritimum*). Tamarisk makes a good windbreak and many tough roses will also cope. To echo the sea's blue try evergreen ceanothus (*Ceanothus* 'Puget Blue' is the bluest), blue cornflowers (*Centaurea cyanus*) and chicory (*Cichorium intybus*), and, for complementary pinks and reds, try self-seeding pink valerian and the wilder geraniums.

WATERSIDE GARDENS

Water lilies, I think, should be chosen to complement the stretches of water in which they are planted and should therefore should not be too flamboyant. I would suggest a soft pink or near-white single flower, except in wilder areas, where whatever is native to your region, such as the yellow *Nuphar lutea*, would suit. Water lilies like a particular depth of water, depending on variety, but none likes really deep water.

In the right setting a bank of arum lilies is highly architectural. Choose *Zantedeschia aethiopica*, pure white and hardy, *Z. aethiopica* 'Green Goddess', also hardy, or *Z.* 'Pink Mist', a very soft blush pink. The last two complement each other – not mixed but, perhaps, planted en masse

in the same pond. Skunk cabbage (*Lysichiton americanus*), with similarly large, arum-like, yellow flowers, is also extremely effective.

Among the water-loving irises I especially favour *Iris foetidissima*, unfairly called the stinking iris, which has browny-ochre flowers in late spring followed in autumn and winter by brilliant red seeds in chunky pods. All year its leaves contribute with texture and shape. *I. chrysographes* has superb black flowers that could come from a Japanese woodblock print. This likes permanently damp soil rather than its tubers in water, as does *I. ensata*: 'Jitsugetsu' and 'Pin Stripe' are both striking named varieties.

Grow spear-leaved irises alongside low-growing hostas. Hostas have really boring flowers, but their flat, heart-shaped leaves provide a good contrast with iris foliage. *H. sieboldiana*, large and imposing with steel-blue leaves, is the parent of many striking hybrids, and *H.* 'Halcyon' is even more steely coloured if planted in shade. Do not be tempted to mix varieties: hostas are far more effective in large swathes of the same type.

TOWN GARDENS

Modern gardens also tend to be spare in their planting, especially beside water. In general – although Helen Dillon's Dublin garden (see pages 142–45) is clearly an exception – town gardens benefit from a controlled palette, as too much busyness reduces the feeling of space (the Dillon garden is about 4000 square metres [almost 1 acre], which is roomy as town gardens go). One garden I know in London, almost filled by two giant plane trees (*Platanus* × *hispanica*), makes do with little but tubs of white arum lilies (*Zantedeschia aethiopica*) spaced beside a still canal. Others take on a Zen calmness with bamboo, preferably *Phyllostachys nigra*, a bamboo that is not too much of a bully, with black culms that are very effective against brickwork or a pale background.

TWENTIETH- AND TWENTY-FIRST-CENTURY DESIGNERS

Sir Geoffrey Jellicoe left his musical canal bare apart from lawns on either side, and another watery area deploys arum lilies at the edges. Ian Hamilton Finlay, like Frank Lloyd Wright, left nature to itself while allowing vistas and eye-catchers to become part of the architecture. Fernando Caruncho takes typically Mediterranean agricultural plants – vines, olives, wheat – and allies them with pencil cypresses to make his designs. Charles Jencks and Kim Wilkie use earth reliefs to make patterns, as did Charles Bridgeman in the eighteenth century, while Modernist designers generally sculpt and mow grass in patterns (an ephemeral variation on this is to make patterns with early morning dew).

WATER GARDENS OPEN TO THE PUBLIC

Gardens are listed alphabetically by name. Opening hours are given only where contact details are not available, and these are subject to change.

Annevoie, 37a rue des Jardins, B-5537 Annevoie, Namur, Belgium
+32 (0)82 679797
info@jardins.dannevoie.be; jardins.dannevoie.be

Claremont, Portsmouth Road, Esher,
Surrey KT10 9JG, England
+44 (0)1372 467806
claremont@nationaltrust.org.uk; nationaltrust.org.uk

Columbine Hall, Stowupland,
Suffolk IP14 4AT, England
+44 (0)1449 612219
info@columbinehall.co.uk; columbinehall.co.uk
Open under Invitation to View Scheme; see
invitationtoview.co.uk

Dillon Garden, 45 Sandford Road, Ranelagh,
Dublin 6, Ireland
info@dillongarden.com; dillongarden.com

Fallingwater, between Mill Run and Ohiopyle,
Pennsylvania, USA
+1 724 329 8501 for tour information

Garden of Cosmic Speculation, Dumfries &
Galloway, Scotland
Open under Scotland's Gardens Scheme; see
gardensofscotland.org. Also open to groups who
apply in writing to Charles A. Jencks, PO Box
31627, London W11 3XB

El Generalife, Granada, Spain
alhambradegranada.org

Giverny, Normandy, France
giverny.org

The Hanbury Garden, La Mortola,
Ventimiglia, Italy

Ilnacullin (Garanish Island), Glengariff, Bantry Bay,
County Cork, Ireland
Mar–Oct

Innisfree, Millbrook, New York 12545, USA
+1 845 677 8000
innisfreegarden.org

Isola Bella, Lake Maggiore, Piedmont, Italy
stresa.net/isole/bella

Jardin Majorelle, Avenue Yacoub el Mansour,
Marrakesh, Morocco
+212 024 301852
jardin.majorelle@menara.ma; jardinmajorelle.com

Little Sparta, Dunsyre, Lanarkshire, Scotland
little_sparta@btinternet.com; littlesparta.org

Ninfa, near Latina, Italy
Limited opening hours; see cisterna.it

Nishat Bagh, Srinagar, Kashmir, India
Sunrise–sunset

Peterhof, St Petersburg, Gulf of Finland, Russia
Tues–Sun 10 am–5 pm (closed first Tues in month)

Schloss Wörlitz, D-06786 Wörlitz, Sachsen-Anhalt,
Germany
Apr and Oct 10 am–4.30 pm (Mon 1–4.30 pm)
May–Sep 10 am–6 pm (Mon 1–6 pm)
Nov–Mar 9 am–3 pm

Shute House, Donhead St Mary, Shaftesbury,
Dorset SP7 9DG, England
+44 (0)1935 828866

Stourhead, Stourton, Warminster, Wiltshire
BA12 6QD, England
+44 (0)1747 841152; +44 (0)870 240 4068 (box
office)
stourhead@nationaltrust.org.uk; nationaltrust.org.uk

Tenryu-ji, Arashiyama, Kyoto, Japan
8.30 am–5.30 pm (closes at 5 pm Nov–Mar)

Trebah, Mawnan Smith, Falmouth, Cornwall
TR11 5JZ, England
+44 (0)1326 252200
mail@trebah-garden.co.uk; trebah-garden.co.uk

Tresco Abbey, Isles of Scilly, England
+44 (0)1720 424108
mikenelhams@tresco.co.uk; tresco.co.uk

Villa d'Este, Tivoli, Italy
+39 0424 464191
info@villadestetivoli.info; villadestetivoli.info

Zhuozheng, Dongbei Street, Suzhou, China
8.15 am–4.15 pm

GARDEN DESIGNERS

George Carter
Silverstone Farm, North Elmham,
Norfolk NR20 5EX, England
+44 (0)1362 668130

Fernando Caruncho
Paseo de Narcea 17, Urbanización Ciudalcampo,
28707 Madrid, Spain
+34 91 657 0051
info@fernandocaruncho.com;
fernandocaruncho.com

Simon Irvine
Simon Irvine Designs, Eklanda Bäck 60,
431 49 Mölndal, Sweden
+46 31 272 330
info@simonirvine.net; simonirvine.net

Charles Jencks
charlesjencks.com

Oehme, van Sweden & Associates
800 G Street SE, Washington, DC 20003, USA
+1 202 546 7575
ovsla.com

Vladimir Sitta, Terragram
105 Reservoir Street, Surry Hills,
NSW 2010, Australia
+61 (0)2 9365 3371

FURTHER READING

Patrick Bowe, *The Gardens of Ireland*, London (Hutchinson) 1986

Christopher Bradley-Hole, *The Minimalist Garden*, London (Mitchell Beazley) 1999

Karl-Dietrich Bühler, *The Scandinavian Garden*, London (Frances Lincoln) 2000

Robert Byron, *The Road to Oxiana*, London (Macmillan) 1937

George Carter, *The New London Garden*, London (Mitchell Beazley) 2000

Beth Chatto, *The Damp Garden*, London (J.M. Dent) 1982

Madison Cox, *Artists' Gardens*, New York (H.N. Abrams) 1993

John Dixon Hunt and Peter Willis (eds), *The Genius of Place*, London (Elek) 1975

Camille Dressler, *Eigg: The Story of an Island*, Edinburgh (Polygon) 1998

Douglas Ellory Pett, *The Parks and Gardens of Cornwall*, Penzance (Alison Hodge) 1998

European Gardens magazine, 1995–96 (*Historic Gardens Review* 1997–)

Nigel Everett, *Wild Gardens: The Lost Desmesnes of Bantry Bay*, Cork (Hafod Press) 2000

Olda FitzGerald, *Irish Gardens*, London (Conran Octopus) 1999

Laurence Fleming and Alan Gore, *The English Garden*, London (Michael Joseph) 1979

The Garden Book, London (Phaidon) 2000

Leslie Geddes-Brown, *The Walled Garden*, London and New York (Merrell) 2007

——, *Waterside Living*, London (Ryland, Peters & Small) 2001

Penelope Hobhouse, *The Story of Gardening*, London (Dorling Kindersley) 2002

Geoffrey Jellicoe, *The Landscape of Civilization*, Northiam (Garden Art Press) 1989

Landscape in Britain 1850–1950, London (Arts Council) 1983

Elizabeth Mavor, *The Grand Tour of William Beckford*, London (Penguin Books) 1986

Cedric Morris, exhib. cat. by Richard Morphet, London (Tate Gallery) 1984

George Plumptre, *The Garden Makers*, London (Pavilion) 1993

Sacheverell Sitwell, *Bridge of the Brocade Sash*, London (Weidenfeld & Nicolson) 1959

Patrick Taylor (ed.), *The Oxford Companion to the Garden*, Oxford (Oxford University Press) 2006

Norah Titley and Frances Wood, *Oriental Gardens*, London (British Library) 1991

Peter Valder, *The Garden Plants of China*, London (Weidenfeld & Nicolson) 1999

James van Sweden, *Gardening with Water*, London (Random House) 1995

Andrew Wilson, *Influential Gardeners*, London (Mitchell Beazley) 2002

PICTURE CREDITS

l: left; r: right; f: far; t: top; b: bottom; c: centre

Aflo 18–19 (Image Kyoto), 24b (Murota Yasuo), 25b (Koichi Sudo), 30–31 (Panoramastock); **Alamy** back jacket tcl (© The National Trust Photolibrary), bcl (© blickwinkel), bcr (© Dennis Cox), br (© Arco Images), 8b (© Wolfgang Kaehler), 20 (© Glow Images), 25tr (© john lander), 28t (© Robert Fried), 28bl (© Panorama Media [Beijing] Ltd.), 28br and 29 (© Dennis Cox), 32t (© dk), 33b (© Mooch Images), 45tr (© Anne-Marie Palmer), 45b (© Colin Walton), 49 (© Roger Turley), 54–55 (© Peter Titmuss), 56t © Robert Harding Picture Library Ltd), 56bl (© Art Kowalsky), 56br (© Arco Images), 57 (© vladphotos), 69b (© The National Trust Photolibrary), 70–71 (©Bildarchiv Monheim GmbH), 72 (© blickwinkel), 73tl and bl (© blickwinkel), 100b (© JUPITERIMAGES/Brand X), 104bl (© RogerPix), 104br (© AA World Travel Library), 110–11 (© Steve Frost), 112l (© isifa Image Service s.r.o.), 113b (© Design Pics Inc.), 114–15 (© Steve Frost), 116 (© scenicireland.com/Christopher Hill Photographic), 117l (© Danita Delimont), 117r (© Scottish Viewpoint); **Arcaid** 146–47 (Reto Guntli); **Peter Baistow** 16br, 17r, 90–91, 93t, br, 94–95, 96–97, 184bl; **Norman Blackburn** (normanblackburn.com) 53l; **Clive Boursnell** 77l, 81b, 106–107, 152, 160l; **The Bridgeman Art Library** 6 (Château du Grand Trianon, Versailles, France), 13b (Private Collection/ Photo © Christie's Images), 14c (Private Collection), 66–67 (© Southampton City Art Gallery, Hampshire), 82–83 (Musée de l'Orangerie, Paris/Lauros/ Giraudon), 85 (Art Gallery and Museum, Kelvingrove, Glasgow, Scotland/© Glasgow City Council [Museums]); ©**British Library Board, All Rights Reserved,** 12 (Or.3714 f.173v) 84bl and br; © **The Trustees of the British Museum** 13 top; **Nicola Browne** 164r; **Fernando Caruncho & Associates S.L./Photo: Laurence Toussaint** 177b; **Peter Cook/VIEW** back jacket bl, 154–55, 157; **Corbis** 14t (© Clay Perry), 33t (© John T. Young), 38–39 (© Earl & Nazima Kowall), 50–51 (© Mark Bolton), 52 (© Yann Arthus-Bertrand), 84t; **Design Press/Lars Hallén** 148l; **Roger Foley** 178–81, 184r, 185; © **Scott Frances/ESTO/VIEW** 156; **John Glover** 77r; **Jerry Harpur** back jacket tcr, 17l (design: Vladimir Sitta), 34–35, 37l and r, 76t, 92, 100t, 101t, 108–109, 120b, 121tr and tl; 124–25, 125tr, 126–27, 132r, 133, 142–45, 148r, 149r, 153, 165, 182–83; **Jeremy Hoare** 22–23, 24t, 25tl; © **Holker Hall** 53r; **innisfree.org** 118–19, 120t and b; **The Interior Archive** 149l (Herbert Ypma); © **Kulturstiftung DessauWörlitz, Bildarchiv** 73tr, cr and br; **Andrew Lawson** back jacket tr, 9t, 9bl, 9br, 14b, 15t, 16tl, 60t, 93bl, 122–23, 125br, 128l, 138–41, 150–51, 158–59, 160–61, 161tr; **Le Scanff-Mayer** back jacket tl, 2–3, 42–43, 44, 45tl, 46–48;

Alain Le Toquin 174–75, 176–77, 176b; **Marianne Majerus** 8t, 11, 16tr, 62–65, 112–13, 130–31, 132l, 134–37; **National Gallery of Scotland** 69t; **Clive Nichols** 21tr, 76b, 128r, 129, 162–63, 184tl, 186; © **NTPL** 13br (Ian Shaw), 15b (Mike Williams), 21tl (Andrew Butler), 68 (Andrew Butler), 74–75 (Derek Croucher), 78–79 (Colin Clarke), 80 (John Bethell), 81t (Derek Croucher); **PanoramaStock/Robert Harding** 26–27, 32b; **Photolibrary Group** 40 (Gary Rogers), 164l (Ron Sutherland), 187; **Courtesy of the Powerscourt Estate** 7; **Will Pryce** 166–67, 168, 169tr and br; **Alex Ramsay** front jacket, 58–59, 60b, 61, 86–89, 102–103, 104tl and tr, 105; **Per Ranung** 169tl and bl; **Gary Rogers/The Garden Collection** 41; **Ianthe Ruthven** 161bl and br, 170–71, 172, 173t, bl and br; © **Ryland, Peters & Small/Loupe Images/Jan Baldwin** 98–99, 101b; **V&A** 36.

The publishers have made every effort to trace and contact copyright holders of the illustrations reproduced in this book; they will be happy to correct in subsequent editions any errors or omissions that are brought to their attention.

189